Granny Panty Chronicles

Tales of Dating Mistakes, Heartbreaks, and the Faith that Carries You Through

Carrie Lea

Granny Panty Chronicles
Copyright © 2025 by Carrie Lea. All rights reserved.

This is a work of nonfiction. The stories shared here are based on the author's personal experiences and recollections, told to the best of her knowledge and memory. To protect the privacy of individuals, names and identifying details have been changed.

Author photograph by melshanicolephotography.com

ISBN-13: 979-8-218-76542-2

Book Cover Design and Interior Formatting by 100Covers.

To my mommy, my biggest supporter and best cheerleader.

Thank you for believing in me and seeing me as an author before I did.

There is nothing like a praying mother.

Table of Contents

Introduction vii

Chapter 1: Confidence by Way of
Vaseline and a Mother's Love 1

Chapter 2: Serial Dating, Sunday School,
and Sweet Love 8

Chapter 3: College, Confusion, and
The Red Flags I Ignored 18

Chapter 4: Cuddles, Chemistry, and Compromising 26

Chapter 5: When Moving for Love
Becomes a Lesson in Letting Go 36

Chapter 6: No Sex, No Problem . . . Right? 46

Chapter 7: When God Says Not Yet 56

Chapter 8: Online Dating: Proof God Has a
Sense of Humor 70

Chapter 9: Over Before it Even Starts 83

Chapter 10: Unexpected Answers to Prayers – Part 1 86

Chapter 11: Unexpected Answers to Prayers – Part 2......... 105

Chapter 12: Where do I Draw the Panty Line?................... 116

Chapter 13: Am I The Drama?... 133

Chapter 14: Cuffing Season, Bad Advice, and
Leftover Chicken Wings... 150

Chapter 15: What do a Salon, a Car
Accident, and an Uber Driver Have in Common?............... 165

Chapter 16: From Love Drought to Love Downpour......... 181

Chapter 17: Don't Settle for Saul.. 190

Epilogue 199

Acknowledgements 201

Introduction

Welcome.

I'll be honest, hospitality is not my strength. But something about what you're about to read makes me feel like I should be offering you a beverage. This is personal—like inviting you into my home and hoping you don't notice the scuffed floorboards.

But now that you're here, come in. Kick off your shoes. Find a comfortable spot on the couch.

And get ready. Get ready to nod and say "mmhmm." Get ready to side-eye me and maybe learn from my mistakes—so you don't make the same ones. Get ready to feel something—because as I share my stories, I have a feeling you'll see pieces of your own.

Among Christian singles, you'll often hear the classic line: *I'm just letting God write my love story.* As if we've all agreed He's holding the pen, and we're along for the plot twists.

I remember learning about this concept from a young Christian couple in their twenties. They each shared how they had sworn off dating, started walking in obedience, and within months—boom, God had knitted their hearts together.

How sweet (*insert deep eyeroll here*).

Naturally, I had similar expectations when I handed over the pen and vowed to let Jesus write the story of my love life. I even had a preferred timeline. I figured if I was obedient long enough, He'd get right to work. After all, the Bible says, "Ask and it shall be given unto you." I was asking and doing what I thought was the right thing, so I expected to see the goodness of the Lord in the land of the living... by the end of the year

(*Stop laughing.*)

What I didn't realize when I echoed the cliché "I'm letting God write my love story" was that it meant surrendering *every* part of my life to Him—including my underwear drawer.

I invited God to reshape my approach to intimacy through boundaries, love, and correction. That meant trading in my sexy skivvies for some full-coverage granny panties out of a desire to protect the heart He was healing. No more seductive rendezvous that left me broken or confused. Instead, I started showing up for faith-filled appointments where God could rewrite my understanding of romance, desire, and His design for dating.

Trusting Jesus with the most personal parts of my life—especially my dating life—often felt like stepping into a dark room, blindfolded, clutching His promises like a lifeline. I could make my own plans to navigate or escape that room, but when I insisted on doing it my way, I ended up tripping over obstacles I never expected to see—hurting myself and others in the process.

All along, He was standing there, hand extended—ready to guide me through. But that could only happen when I stopped fighting for control and let His Light lead the way.

You may have picked up this book because you want to feel more confident in your dating life. Or you're simply looking for some camaraderie in this dating journey that's peppered with swipes, sliding in DMs, and plain ol' weird encounters.

But let me be clear: this isn't a book of dating dos and don'ts.

It's a book about the art of waiting and how God will use our desires to bring us closer to Him, leading us through an inevitable journey of faith, self-awareness, and trust.

As you read each story, you'll notice I changed the names of the people involved. Not to bash or belittle any of the men mentioned because this isn't about them. You'll see my mess just as much as you'll see theirs. My hope is that you'll walk away with wisdom and an understanding about how to navigate the swirl of emotions that come with unexpected seasons—along with a fresh desire to bring God into every aspect of your dating story.

Because waiting on God to write your love story? It's not passive. It's a bold, everyday act of faith. If you don't see yourself in these pages, simply pause and observe. Ask how you might extend grace, mercy, and love to someone else, because you never know what part of their journey they are on and what role you may play in one of the God-written chapters of their life.

Get ready to talk love and lust, heartache and healing—and best of all, boundaries and belief.

Chapter 1

Confidence by Way of Vaseline and a Mother's Love

I read an article once that said a girl's confidence peaks at the age of nine.

At first, I guffawed at that statistic. It seemed like an unhappy fact.

If nine years old is the most confident I'll ever be without experience, accolades, or the beauty in discovering life—what a sad thing, right?

But the more I sat with it, the more I realized that nine years old might actually be the last age before the world tries to steal the joy and truth that we are fearfully and wonderfully made.

At nine, my thoughts were focused on playing with my cousins on Saturday nights before church, coordinating my outfits with my glasses, and getting lost in whatever book I was reading.

But nine was also the first time my confidence, especially in how I saw my rich, dark skin, was threatened by someone else's standards.

Monday through Friday, I rode the bus and sat in my assigned seat. Across the aisle sat Staring Stanley. He was a year older than I and got on the bus two or three stops before I did.

One day, as I sat in my assigned seat, legs swinging and my jherri curl shining *(don't laugh, my mommy said it helped my hair grow)*, I felt Staring Stanley's eyes on me.

I glanced across the aisle, and sure enough—there he was. Squinted eyes locked on mine, a slight scowl on his face. He pointed his pudgy finger in my direction and said,

"You ugly. You ugly becuz you black and got dark skin."

I blinked, stunned. I couldn't even comprehend what he was saying.

My skin was the same deep, dark hue as my mother, father, my brother, a slew of my cousins, aunts, and uncles. I took pride in the rich chocolate tones passed down from our family's gene pool. I loved how our skin glistened on warm, sunny days, freshly lathered in Vaseline—because in our family, being dark-skinned and ashy was a cardinal sin.

I found my entire family beautiful. And my daddy? He repeatedly told me how pretty I was and he wasn't a liar. So, in my nine-year-old mind, I simply could not grasp how the most obvious and admirable part of me could suddenly make me ugly.

But Staring Stanley said it with such conviction and anger that, for a second. I wondered—had I misunderstood what beauty really was?

I needed answers. I needed truth. And I knew exactly who to ask.

The moment the school bus dropped me off, I sprinted up the driveway, tears threatening to spill. I burst through our front door, out of breath, on a mission.

I had to talk to my mommy. Mrs. Gloria T., mommy extraordinaire, was a truth-teller and I needed her truth now.

I didn't grow up with childhood fairytale characters like Santa Claus, the Easter Bunny, or the Tooth Fairy. No sir, no ma'am. Mommy told no lies. When my sister hit me in the face with her Hello Kitty stuffed animal, sending my loose tooth flying across the bedroom—that tooth went in a baggie or the trash. There was no placing it under the pillow with the hopes of a coin or two in the morning.

When Christmas rolled around, we prayed before tearing into our gifts, thanking the Lord for His provision and celebrating the birth of Jesus. It was His day, after all, and the world changed forever when He came in a manger.

We didn't leave out cookies or stay up late waiting for a big-bellied white dude to shimmy down our chimney. My daddy worked two jobs and my mom picked up a retail job for the holidays to give us the Christmas of our dreams. I knew they were the ones shopping for the gifts under the tree.

And for Easter, ahem—*Resurrection Sunday* for all my Saints, we had a celebratory dinner, but there were no candy-filled baskets or bunny-themed decorations. The only pastels we wore were the fly new suits and dresses with thick sashes, big bows, and ruffled socks completed with a press-n-curl that was coiffed to perfection.

I trusted my mommy to tell me the truth, no matter what. I knew she was the right person to talk to when my standard of beauty was challenged.

She was right where she always was when I came home from school: in the kitchen. My friends went home to after-school snacks, but I came home to delicious, home-cooked meals. My siblings and I would change out of our nice school clothes, throw on our play clothes, wash our hands, and get ready to eat.

But eating and changing clothes had to wait that day.

I marched up to Mommy, my personal truth-teller, tears forming again, and I blurted out what Staring Stanley said: "He said I was ugly because I'm Black and my skin is dark."

Mommy kept right on cooking and didn't miss a beat before she said, "That's not true. You. Are. Beautiful. Your dark skin is beautiful, and don't you ever let anybody tell you different."

That was it. She didn't even look my way or stop preparing dinner.

My mother was not a woman of many words, but when she did speak, it was with truth and conviction. She often taught us, "You have what you say. Speak over yourself. Your words have power." So, when mommy said I was beautiful, there were no ifs, ands, or buts about it.

I was beautiful.

After, just like that, I shrugged. The tears that threatened to fall dried up. I changed my clothes and got ready to eat.

The next morning, I was eager to get on the bus and give Staring Stanley a piece of my mind. I had it all planned: neck roll, hand on my hip, the whole nine.

But when I climbed aboard, his seat was empty. I was so bummed because I had my guns drawn and ready to fire, and as my daddy always says, "Just when you have your guns drawn, there's nothing to shoot."

My bullseye opportunity came that afternoon on our bus ride home.

The moment I spotted Staring Stanley in his seat, I marched straight up to him, stuck my finger in his face and said, "You're a liar. I'm not ugly. I'm beautiful and my dark skin is beautiful." I'm sure I probably rolled my neck a little for emphasis, delivering each word with extra sass. My confidence was at an all-time high.

But what I remember most wasn't what I said—it was his reaction. His eyes widened, and if I didn't know any better, I thought I saw tears gather in the corners of his eyes. He didn't say a word. Just stared at me.

It wasn't the response I expected. Where was the fire he had yesterday? The certainty in his insult? I was prepared to list the reasons why I was beautiful. My smooth skin. My full lips. The nose that was a perfect blend of my parents. My small ears from my daddy. And the shine that came from my well-greased legs (courtesy of Vaseline). I'd even matched my pink glasses to my shirt that day.

"Aren't you going to say something?" I asked. I wanted him to argue so I could prove him wrong and defend the beauty of my skin.

He just turned to me and mumbled, "Okay."

The one detail I hadn't told my mother was what Staring Stanley looked like.

His skin was a few shades darker than mine, a deep, shiny black that glistened like it had diamonds beneath the surface. He had full lips—his bottom one with a pink patch in the middle, surrounded by darker spots, like a wound that never fully healed. He had a broad nose that was the perfect centerpiece to his chubby cheeks and big eyes. And when he smiled, you'd see a jumble of big, awkward teeth still finding their place. It was clear braces were in his future.

He wore pants that were too long, rolled into jumbo cuffs so he wouldn't trip while walking. And he was always tugging at his clothes— pulling a sleeve down, yanking pants up, and dragging his coat on the ground behind him while chewing on a pencil stuck in the corner of his mouth.

I'll never understand why any kid who looked more like me than anyone else on the bus would say something so hurtful. But after our swift exchange, he never said a negative word about my skin or my appearance ever again. Instead of peering over the seat with a scowl, he'd flash a wide, toothy grin then wave and say hello.

The confidence I carried in that moment—as a nine-year-old girl who genuinely loved what she saw in the mirror—is the same confidence I tried to show up with when dating. A confidence that shined from the inside out.

But if I'm honest, that nine-year-old confidence has taken a few hits over the years.

Between career ups and downs, financial woes, challenging friendships, or just a bloated week (or three), dating has often delivered a one-two punch to my self-worth. I mistakenly let my relationship status, or lack thereof, dictate how I saw myself. Instead of believing what God has spoken about me and seeing myself as His beautiful masterpiece, I let the attention (or inattention) from a man chip away at my confidence.

Little did I know, my single season would become the classroom where I'd learn the difference between confidence and God-rooted identity. I would learn not to tie my worth to who pursued me, but to the One who created me.

I had a lot more to learn about love, God, and relationships.

And it all started in the fourth grade.

Dear Diary,

I have a boyfriend!

Well, I don't know if boyfriend is what I would be allowed to call him since we only talk on the phone and see each other at school. In the movies, boyfriends hold your hand and kiss you.

He's cute and shares his chips with me at lunch. He also calls me on the phone. We're not allowed to talk long though.

He told me I was pretty (but I think he told Megan that too.)

When we got off the phone on Friday, Mommy asked me who the "lil' boy" I've been talking to was.

I told her his name is Jay and he's white. She said I'm too young to have a boyfriend.

I thought she might have an issue with Jay being white, but she just said, "Me and your daddy just care that you're as welcome in his home as he would be here."

When I see him on Monday, I'm going to walk up to him and ask, "Does your mommy know I'm Black, and can I come over to your house?

If he didn't say yes, I was going to dump him and wait for R.J. to ask me to be his girlfriend.

If R.J. is with Erica, I think Chris or Reggie will be fine.

I like having boyfriends.

Chapter 2

Serial Dating, Sunday School, and Sweet Love

Hi, I'm Carrie (*you say,* "*Hi Carrie*"), and I was a serial dater.

According to my good friend, Google, a serial dater is someone who loves the thrill of the chase and the excitement of the early stages of dating someone new. They typically jump ship before anything too serious develops, and pride themselves on the power to leave one person and start fresh with another.

What Google *doesn't* mention is this: Serial daters often jump ship because they are afraid of being hurt ... or simply because they don't know how to be alone.

Looking back at my early dating chronicles, I realize I displayed traits of both a serial dater and serial monogamist. Serial monogamists, for the record, are most comfortable in committed relationships. They move from one to the next with little to no time in between—rarely sitting in a season of singleness or casually dating just to get to know someone.

That was me. I always preferred a solid relationship over random dating. The goal was to be in love (and not to be alone). Granted, I probably can't count anything before ninth grade as a relationship, especially in the 90's when "dating" mostly meant seeing someone at school and bonding over R&B lyrics that we were too young to understand. *(can't you just hear the Boyz II Men harmonizing in the background, "nahooo?")*.

High school was when I had my first real boyfriend.

At the tender age of 14, I fell in love with Rapping Richard. He was tall, broad-shouldered, with deep chocolate skin, a sweet smile, and a fake New York accent. He had the softest lips that glistened whenever he licked them (which he often did while talking to me).

(Swoon.)

He was one year older, and his dream in life was to become a famous rap star someday.

Compared to Rapping Richard, my elementary school crushes and middle school "boos" didn't even come close. We'd talk for hours on the phone—until my dad would pick up the phone in another room and say, "That's enough," which, of course, led to a quick goodbye.

When we weren't on the phone, his bubbly cursive handwriting filled pages and pages of notes he'd hand me in between classes as we navigated the bustling hallways of high school. My stomach would flutter the moment I saw him waiting by my locker or outside my classroom in his baggy jeans and wrinkled polos. He'd flash that bright smile at me and everything—and everyone would disappear.

After school, he'd walk me to cheerleading or track practice. We'd hold hands, steal quick kisses, and stroll as slowly as possible, trying to stretch each minute together. If he didn't have to be home right away, he would wait for me after practice until my mom arrived to pick me up.

Since I wasn't technically allowed to kiss—or even be alone with Rapping Richard yet, we had a silent system in place. The moment was saw my mom's car rounding the corner of the school parking lot, we'd part ways. He'd head in the opposite direction, stealing glances to smile or blow me a kiss. If my mom ever connected the boy lingering around school with the voice over the house phone in a five-person household during the pre-cell phone era, she never said anything.

And I didn't bring it up either.

I wasn't ready for the sermon about why I wasn't allowed to be close to a boy yet.

Sermons were a regular occurrence in my life growing up in an old-school, foot-stomping, handclapping, lap-running, tambourine-playing, tongue-speaking, predominantly Black Apostolic Pentecostal church. While it laid a foundation for knowing Jesus Christ, it was also steeped in tradition and legalistic rules that clouded my view of sex, dating, and Jesus.

My father worked part-time at the church and served as Sunday School Superintendent, so it was completely normal for us to be at church multiple times a week—and always on Sundays.

Sunday was a full-blown marathon.

It started with Sunday School, where everyone was split up into different rooms to discuss various aspects of the Bible. Kids were grouped by grade level, and adults by age, life stage, or preferred teaching style.

After Sunday school, we had a small break before the main service began. During that time, everyone gathered to enjoy homemade baked goods: no-bake cheesecake, sweet potato pie, yellow cake with chocolate icing, or pound cake—all prepared and served by the mothers and grandmothers of the church.

The elders sat around rows of tables in the church basement, dressed in their 80s-style Sunday suits with oversized, tinted glasses and shiny jheri-curls. The younger kids ran wild, thrilled to be free of anything resembling school. Meanwhile, the teenagers crowded around the makeshift candy store, buying Lemon Heads, Now-n-Laters, Jolly Ranchers, or Boston Baked Beans. (*Why they allowed young kids to get hyped up on sugar before a super-long church service, I'll never know.*)

Then came the main event—Sunday service.

Announcements. The formal choir entrance. Testimonials. Prayers. Songs. Church offering (also known as the unofficial church fashion show). And of course, praise breaks that could go on indefinitely. Thankfully, whether we were mid-sermon or not, my father gathered up the family for a prompt exit at 1:30 p.m. on the dot. On days I knew my mother was fixing one of my favorite Sunday suppers, I would quietly count down the minutes in anticipation—hoping we wouldn't have to come back for Sunday evening service.

In our tradition-driven church culture, women were only allowed to wear dresses or skirts. Makeup and jewelry were signs of immorality. We were taught about the grace of God, but mostly through the lens of fearing the fire and brimstone of hell. The message was clear: to stay out of hell, you needed to give your life to God, follow the traditions, and never sin.

But woven into these man-made traditions was the truth of the Bible that pierced my heart as a twelve-year-old pre-teen. That's when I first decided to give my life to Jesus.

That Sunday, my parents were out of town, and my older siblings were tasked with ensuring the three of us went to church. Even in their absence, there was no question—we were expected to be there.

We sat in the back of the sanctuary partly to have proof that we were there and partly because my brother and sister were too old to join me in children's church. Our Assistant Pastor, Elder M, preached a powerful message about loving God and keeping his commandments. And miraculously, the altar call started *before* 1:30 p.m. that day.

Altar call always scared me.

At that age, I was still shy around people outside of my immediate family. The thought of walking down the center aisle of the sanctuary with everyone's eyes on me to declare my love for Jesus was terrifying. I secretly admired the teenagers and young adults who made their way to the front and proclaimed their love with a parent or caregiver at their side. But me? I figured I could just pull someone to the side later and whisper in their ear, "I want to be closer to Jesus," and skip the public display. Besides, the drama of alter calls didn't help ease the fear. People would burst into tears or fall to the floor. Then the church mothers would rush in with a maroon-colored cloth to gently cover them up.

I worried that if I didn't cry or faint or shake uncontrollably, maybe I wouldn't be doing it "right."

As the choir softly hummed the hymn, "Take me to the water," the familiar feeling of unrest danced in the pit of my stomach. I had sat through countless altar calls, but lately, something had been stirring inside of me each time. I wanted to show God how much I appreciated Him sending His only Son to die for me. And I knew the only way to do that was to proclaim my love for Him. Elder M extended his right hand toward the congregation and said, "Won't you come?"

It felt like he was speaking directly to me. My pulse quickened. My heart pounded. And that's when an inner battle broke loose.

> You know if you go down there, you'll never be able to have fun again.
> *Come to me.*
> All your friends will think you're weird.
> *Answer my call.*
> What is the point of being baptized? Your brother and sister are ready to go and are going to be mad that you made them stay after service. You need your parents' permission any ol' way.
> *I AM all you need.*

I sat on my hands and glanced at my sister, wondering if she heard the voices too. I stayed seated, hoping the feeling would fade. I wasn't bold enough to walk down the aisle on my own.

I lowered my head and hot tears streamed down my cheeks.

Then Elder M said, "Don't miss your moment. God is calling you now."

Come to me, Carrie.

I nudged my sister and rose from my seat. She looked annoyed at first, until she saw the tears in my eyes. She stood, took my hand, and walked me down to the altar. By the time I reached the front, I was a blubbering mess. Between sobs, I prayed and confessed my love for Jesus. I told Him I believed He died on the cross for me and rose from the grave.

After my confession, a wave of peace and warmth spread from the top of my head to the soles of my feet. The combative voice in my mind went silent, and I knew I had made the right decision. My sister smiled at me before handing me over to one of the altar workers. I was led into a side room to change into the baptism attire.

After being baptized, I couldn't wait to tell my parents I had given my life to God. I hoped they'd be proud that I finally answered the call.

That night, I went to bed full of joy and anticipation, eager to wake up and see what life would be like as a newly saved church girl.

But the next morning, I woke up in a silent panic. Lying in bed, I was hit by a flurry of whispered lies—echoes of the strict, man-made traditions that magnified everything I couldn't do.

What did you go and do that for?
Now, you can't do any of the things you like to do.
Saved folks don't have fun.
You can't listen to music, dance, or hang out with your friends.
You'll be a big disappointment to God.
You should quit before you get started.

I stared at the ceiling; my joy now tangled with worry.

Had my newfound freedom in Christ just handcuffed me from everything that brought me joy? I loved dancing to Janet Jackson in my bedroom. Was that a sin now? What about when

I secretly ate Kool-Aid candy in my room— did that count as a sin, too?

I was too young and too new in my walk with God to know that the enemy's lies weren't true. I didn't realize it was simply a tactic, a sneaky strategy meant to discourage young believers before they could grow strong in their faith. My spiritual immaturity tried to reason through the accusations, but eventually I gave in. As the years passed, I drifted away from holy living. I had the misconception that everything enjoyable was a sin—including kissing boys. And honestly, kissing boys was way too fun for me to want to give it up.

My mom, always the truth-teller, once warned me: "Kissing leads to sex."

Now as an adult, I wholeheartedly agree. But as a teenager desperate for those stolen moments with her boyfriend, it felt a little dramatic. At the time, Rapping Richard and I were an item. We were inseparable, at least after school. And kissing felt completely normal based on what I knew.

Then one weekend, while out of town with my father for a church event, I came home to heartbreaking news.

Rapping Richard had cheated on me.

My sister had seen him at the movies walking hand-in-hand with his so-called best friend. She told my parents, who then sat me down and said I was no longer allowed to see him because he had taken another girl out on a date.

Talk about emotional teen trauma. I'm not sure what's worse: finding out you've been cheated on, or having your parents be the ones to break the news. Either way, it was a gut punch that knocked the wind out of me.

My life had officially become a real-life Judy Blume novel. I was knee-deep in teenage anguish, pouring my soul into a floral diary with a matching pen, furiously scribbling questions like:

Why would my sister tell my parents first instead of telling me?
Was it really true or had she somehow been mistaken?
Was it my Rapping Richard at the movies?
Were they really holding hands, or did they accidentally brush fingers?
And why did my dad sound like he'd suspected Rapping Richard's lies all along?
What would my friends say?
Most importantly, what was this devastating feeling that made me want to cry and smash things at the same time?

Heartbreak.

This was my first foray into heartbreak. Every experience or miniscule "relationship" before this had ended quickly—and I was usually the one doing the breaking up. We'd both move on to new crushes or the next school rumor within a week. Nothing had ever cut this deep. But this was different. It was unexpected. It was humiliating. And it hurt.

I knew what I had to do.

Because let's be honest—this was high school. Everyone knew everything about everybody's relationship. If someone sneezed wrong on a date, the whole school heard about it by third period.

I had to break up with Rapping Richard.

Dear Diary,

I feel so torn. I can't believe Rapping Richard cheated on me. What was he thinking? And he kept denying it! But my sister saw it with her own eyes. He wasn't even smart enough to do it in a less popular movie theatre. Ugh. Boys are so dumb.

I need to break up with him because I don't tolerate that behavior. I hate to admit it, but if I break up with him, I'll miss him. He said he's sorry and he even cried! I just don't think I can forgive him—tears or no tears.

I heard a saying once that said, "You teach people how to treat you."

I think he needs to learn the lesson quick, fast, and in a hurry, and see that I can move on without him. Is that mean?

I don't think so.

I know—I'll go out with Driving Dante. That will teach him.

I can't wait to share my plan with my friends. He'll regret the day he ever cheated on me.

Chapter 3

College, Confusion, and The Red Flags I Ignored

I broke up with Rapping Richard and immediately started going out with another high school boy who owned a car. That meant real dates, not just lingering by lockers or hanging out after school. He was cute, but his sloppy kisses had me missing Rapping Richard more than I wanted to admit. The fling fizzled out quickly, leaving just enough room for me to let Rapping Richard back in.

Rapping Richard stuck around through my freshman year of college and well into the spring of my sophomore year. But things shifted after I pledged a sorority.

It just happened to be the same sorority his mother belonged to. Once she found out I was pledging, she told him while I was standing directly beside him, "She's about to leave you."

I guffawed. He didn't believe her. I couldn't believe she said it with me standing right there.

But she was right.

Within weeks of joining, it was as if my eyes were open. I could see all the "new-boo" potential I now had access to—not just on my campus, but at other universities within driving distance.

At one of the many parties I now frequented, a sorority sister from a neighboring school introduced me to one of our fraternity brothers, a close friend of hers, whom I'll call Smitten Steven.

Smitten Steven, also known as Smitty Stevie, was a pre-law student, impeccably stylish, soft-spoken, slightly mysterious, and undeniably attractive. His smooth, dark chocolate complexion and sharp features made him look like he'd stepped straight out of a magazine. He had seen a picture of me in her dorm room and was already smitten. The moment I laid eyes on him, the feeling quickly became mutual.

He knew I had a boyfriend but that didn't concern him the slightest. After all, Rapping Richard was not at my school, and he certainly wasn't the one I was spending hours talking to in the wee hours of the morning on Black Planet—the 90s mashup of Black Twitter and MySpace (*where my screen name was, for the record, Chocolate D-lite*).

Smitten Steven was the polar opposite of Rapping Richard, and I was more than intrigued. He had a car, a job, and a real plan for his future. And he was already asking to take me out on dates. Meanwhile, Rapping Richard was riding the bus, writing songs in his momma's house, and choosing underground rap concerts over showing up at my sorority's parties.

One night, as I sat in front of my glowing computer screen, Smitty Stevie asked the question that would seal the deal for Rapping Richard's fate.

Smitty Stevie: So, does your man know you're spending all this time talking to me?

Chocolate D-lite: Not really. But I don't think he's too concerned with that right now.

SS: What makes you think that? I would be more than concerned if my lady were giving her frat brother all her late-night attention.

CD: If he really wanted my attention, he would be trying to have it.

SS: It sounds like he's missing out. Either that or I'm being used.

CD: You don't believe that.

SS: You're right. His loss is my gain. When can I see you and not have to be concerned about your boyfriend?

CD: I have to go home in a couple weeks to get my hair done. I'll be a single woman by then.

SS: I have to see you.

At the same time I was making plans to meet Smitty Stevie at his off-campus apartment, about an hour north of my hometown—I was also making plans to break things off with Rapping Richard the next morning. I didn't want to hurt him more than I already had.

When I called him, he was unavailable because he was in the studio again. He had quit his job recently because they didn't understand his need for "studio time." He and his brother had poured months of effort into producing a music showcase. Every spare dollar and minute went into making music. Which also meant for months, he'd rarely had the money or time to take the bus to my campus to see me.

The end was inevitable.

When we finally spoke, an unexpected wave of emotion washed over me as I told him I didn't think this was working out. Deep down, I'd known the relationship was ending long before Smitty Stevie had entered the picture. (*Dang his momma and her wise predictions.*) His presence and Rapping Richard's absence just made the choice easier.

After we got off the phone, I cried into my pillow. The tears stayed with me for the rest of the evening. Surprisingly, I felt more emotional than I expected. Yes, he'd been part of my life since I was fourteen, but with someone else now capturing my attention, I didn't expect to feel so torn.

As I cried myself to sleep that night, I realized my tears were more of a release. I had been carrying guilt concerning talking with Smitten Steven while still in a relationship with Rapping Richard. While I didn't see a future with Rapping Richard, he was still a sweet, genuine young man with a dream to be a superstar. I had no interest in being a rap star's girlfriend, but I did want to treat him fairly. Properly ending things was the right thing to do, and it freed me to pursue something new.

Wrong as it was, part of me, albeit a tiny part, felt our ending was a justified retribution for the heartbreak he'd caused me back in high school.

From there, I went all in with Smitten Steven. Considering all I knew was relationships, I went straight into relationship mode with him. Our first weekend together was steamy—and it only got steamier from there.

I surprised myself with how quickly I jumped into bed with him. Rapping Richard received the sexually curious teenager who wanted to understand why something that made her body light up was so forbidden in her religious upbringing. I was eager to experience the mechanics of sex, but had an inner consciousness about sin that kept Rapping Richard at bay until I was seventeen years old. However, as a budding twenty-year-old, I threw caution to the wind with Smitty Stevie. He received the more experienced, confident young lady who had suppressed the idea of sin once she realized that she didn't immediately burst into flames after having premarital sex. And since there was a clinic that supplied free birth control, the fear of unwedded pregnancy was much lower than it had once been.

Smitty Stevie did everything I thought a boyfriend should do. He brought me flowers, took me out on nice dates, complimented my smile, and told me about how he loved my dark skin and curly hair. He fit seamlessly into my college world: fraternity and sorority parties, dorm rooms, midterms, and late-night study sessions. He dressed with a maturity beyond most guys our age, carrying himself with a debonair air that always caught my eye. When he met my parents, I think they were just as smitten with him. He was nothing like my previous relationship, and that was a selling point in their eyes.

Smitty Stevie and I were hot and heavy for the spring semester and all through summer. His friends knew about me and my friends knew all about him. We'd make eyes at each other across crowded parties, then slip away together.

But then...he started disappearing. A day. Sometimes two. No calls. No returned texts. After one time too many, I confronted him.

"What is going on with you?"

"What do you mean?" he asked quietly, shoulders slumped, head hung low.

"Why do you just disappear like that?"

"Because I can, it's not like we're together."

The sting of his words slapped me across my face. Not because they were mean but because they were true. Somewhere along the way, I'd gone into full-on relationship mode without us ever making it official. He never said we were exclusive. I just assumed we were because we acted like it.

He invited me to his college graduation where I met all his family. We held hands, kissed, and cuddled in public. I slept with him. I brought him lunch at his new job. He bought me thoughtful gifts and always made me feel special and appreciated.

In my mind, this was a relationship.

In his mind, it wasn't.

"Remember what my uncle told me?" He turned and looked me in my eyes. "I need to see a woman in all four seasons before I make her *my* woman."

I remembered the conversation very clearly. We'd been sitting in the car after dinner, a new neo-soul artist playing in the background. Smitty Stevie told me I was everything he'd ever wanted, but his uncle advised him to experience a woman through all four seasons before committing to her.

In hindsight, I should have waved the red flag right then. Considering the source, and how convenient it was for Smitty Stevie to suddenly cling to this advice, it was suspect at best. Yet Smitten Steven took his words to heart, using them as a built-in excuse to avoid commitment until we dated for at least a year.

If I were hearing this story from any other woman, I would have told her to run in the opposite direction. Any man who is unclear about you is being very clear. He. Does. Not. Want. You. Either that or you're not the only one. Either way, exit stage left. Expeditiously.

But instead, I stayed. What I had thought I had was a relationship was actually a situationship. My mind started racing. I quickly started putting two and two together. I remembered the times Smitty Stevie disappeared for a weekend back on his old college campus, or the time he casually mentioned that an "old friend" of his was in town and they hung out for a bit. I never questioned who the friend was, but now the dots were connecting.

Determined not to get played or hurt any further, I pulled back. I created some much-needed distance between us, both physically and emotionally. And to expedite that process, I decided to return to campus for the big pre-school-starting-slash-end-of-summer party weekend.

Little did I know, another situationship was waiting for me there.

Dear Diary,

I don't know what's going on, but Smitty Stevie is tripping. After all the time we have spent together, he's acting like we're not in a relationship. Excuse me? So what have we been doing for the past few months?

Bet. I'll remember that when he's trying to be up in my face.

Real talk, my feelings are hurt. And I feel stupid. I hate when someone makes a fool out of me. Never. Again. This is what I get for rushing into things with that dude.

Lesson learned. If he doesn't want to take this seriously, I won't either.

I have officially stopped all the relationship stuff. Good thing school is about to start because we won't be in each other's faces. I'll have other things (and hopefully, guys) to occupy my mind and my time.

Chapter 4

Cuddles, Chemistry, and Compromising

There was a lively hum buzzing through campus in anticipation of students returning for the fall semester. You could spot the freshmen who had arrived early for summer programs—they walked with a practiced cockiness meant to mask the intimidation they felt as upperclassmen descended back on campus.

One evening, some of my sorority sisters and I decided to kick it with our campus fraternity brothers before heading to the local hangout. We swapped stories about our summer vacations, boring internships, epic pool parties, and who was now dating who.

I was sitting on the couch when one of the guys plopped down right on my lap and started cracking jokes. I'd seen him around before but hadn't paid much attention. All I knew was he pledged his fraternity, the same one as Smitten Steven, right before I joined my sorority.

"Now that you're technically my sister, I should have your number."

Before I could respond, he grabbed my neon green cell phone and started pressing buttons. I rolled my eyes and held my hand out.

"Yeah, that's not how this works. Get off me, dude." I tried to push him off my lap.

"Am I too heavy?" He teased, wiggling around and trying to make himself weigh more.

I laughed, knocked him off my lap, and stood to go into another room. "I'm a big girl. I can handle it." I said over my shoulder.

The following week I officially moved into my single-occupancy dorm room as the CommUnity Educator (CUE) of my dorm. This was a role where I received free room and board to educate the students in my dorm about cultural differences amongst their peers. At our predominantly white institution (PWI), the program's goal was to promote diversity and build awareness through campus events and programming.

I was still talking with Smitten Steven, but ever since our "four seasons" talk, things had shifted. Between my CUE role, the demands of my journalism degree, and my sorority responsibilities, my schedule was jam-packed. I reclaimed my time and revoked my girlfriend duties from a guy who didn't even consider me his girlfriend. If he noticed, he didn't let on. Instead, he started being more consistent—calling more often, showing up more, and making a greater effort to see me.

"When can I come see you?" he asked one day when I returned to my dorm after my last class.

"Don't you have to work?" I deflected.

"Yeah, but I have some free time this weekend."

"Got it. This weekend won't work. I have an event to host in my dorm but next week will work."

"I miss you, baby. I don't think I can wait that long. Remember when we used to talk all night online? I wanna get back to that."

"You pass out at like ten these days."

Smitten Steven worked what I considered a "real job" where he had to be up early and wear business casual clothing. I was a night owl.

"Babe, that's only because I have to be up so early for work. That doesn't mean I don't miss talking to you."

"Well, let me get through this weekend, okay?"

"You miss me?"

I didn't quite know how to respond. I did miss parts of him, but with the shift in our pseudo-relationship, I had erected a wall to keep from getting hurt.

"I do." I missed the attention he gave me.

"That doesn't sound very convincing."

"I'll show you when you come down."

"That's my girl." I could hear his smile through the phone. "Okay, well, let me let you get back to studying."

I hung up and went to take a shower. On my way back to my room, I heard my phone ringing and rushed to answer, thinking my friends were calling with plans for the night.

"C Lea!" a voice boomed with over-the-top enthusiasm the second I picked up. "What you doing?"

"Who is this?" I asked, caught off guard by the familiarity.

"Don't act like you don't remember me, girl." He laughed and it instantly clicked— Energetic Edward. The same guy who had sat on my lap a few weeks ago and messed with my phone. I laughed and shook my head.

"So, you stalking me now?" I asked.

"Of course not. Just checking in to see how my sister-now-friend is doing?" His charisma practically oozed through the phone, and despite myself, I smiled.

"I just got out of the shower. Gimme a sec." I'm not sure why I was willing to talk but his bright laugh and playful tone were a welcome shift in my mood.

"Girl, don't be over there sharing all your business. How was your day?" That one question led to an hour-long conversation, and then another a few days later. Soon it became a regular thing. Every few evenings, Energetic Edward would call, and we'd swap jokes, compare our favorite (and least favorite) professors, trade the latest campus gossip, and talk about the hottest upcoming parties.

This pattern continued for weeks.

When we crossed paths on campus or at parties, we'd wave from across the room or share a quick hug. He'd ask how my latest assignment went; I'd check in on his group project.

"What's up with you and E?" a friend asked one night.

"What? What do you mean?" I looked at her—surprised. It hadn't occurred to me that anyone was paying attention to my new friendship with Energetic Edward.

"I've seen the way that man looks at you."

"Girl, please. I don't know what you're talking about. We're just friends. You know I'm still kicking it with Smitty Stevie."

"Aw, okay. When was the last time you saw him?"

"He came down not too long ago."

Things with Smitten Steven were…steady, but the smitten feeling was starting to fade on my end. Our schedules rarely lined up anymore, and when I was free to talk or hang out, he was sleeping or hanging with his friends. The fun things we used to do felt like they'd happened years ago instead of just a few months back.

"When are y'all hanging out again?"

"I don't know. I'm sure we'll figure something out."

"Yeah, he better because looks like someone else is moving in on his territory."

I brushed off her last comment, but her words stuck with me. Was Energetic Edward looking at me as more than a friend and I was oblivious? He was friendly with everyone, buzzing around and talking with everybody. He flirted with plenty of girls. He had never said anything inappropriate to me or even hinted he wanted more than friendship.

That is one of the reasons I enjoyed talking to him; there was no pressure, no pretense, no expectations. Conversations with him felt easy, like talking with one of my girls. He made me laugh, and that was just his personality.

Besides, he had a girlfriend. And while Smitten Steven wasn't my boyfriend, I didn't want to be that girl—the one known around campus for hopping from one guy to the next. Also, if I were honest, I had grown attached to Smitty Stevie. I thought there was marriage potential there. We weren't far from his so-called "four seasons" timeframe, and if I didn't know better, I'd say he seemed to be more interested in me since I'd left for school.

The last time we were together, I thought he was about to say those magical three words. Fearing I wouldn't be able to say it back, I cracked a joke to change the subject. He didn't find the joke that funny, but when I told Energetic Edward the same one, he thought it was hilarious.

Eventually, my phone calls with Energetic Edward became a nightly ritual. Each conversation grew more personal. He told me about his childhood, his first heartbreak, and how he had no idea what he wanted to do with his degree once he graduated. I shared stories about my family, funny memories from high school, and a tale about my high school sweetheart including how Smitten Steven came on the scene.

I started looking forward to his calls each night or hoping I would spot him at the local bar or student hangout. I'd walk in the room and immediately scan it to see if he was there.

One weeknight, he asked me if I wanted to hang out. I did—but I wasn't sure if I should. In college, "hanging out" usually meant sitting in someone's house, having a drink, or watching a movie. Considering our growing friendship and the questions people had already started asking about us, there was an unspoken agreement to keep this, whatever this was, semi-private.

We knew each other's significant others by association. We had even shared a couple grievances about what we wished they would do more of or better, but had never crossed the line into badmouthing them.

Once we decided to hang out at his place, he picked me up outside my dorm. His big grin met me first as I climbed into the car.

"What do you want to listen to, Jodeci or Lil' Kim?"

I knew Jodeci would set a very different mood than I intended for the evening, so I replied, "Put that Lil' Kim on."

He sped down the street while Lil' Kim's explicit lyrics spewed out the car's speakers. We sang along to the hooks, throwing in exaggerated dance moves, laughing the whole way. The laughter followed us into his apartment, which he shared with three other guys. He had the basement to himself while the others lived upstairs.

Since it was our first time hanging out, we stayed in the main living room. As I sat down on their couch, he threw his legs over my lap and sat much closer than I expected.

"I'm a cuddler," he said with a shrug as I gave him a surprised look.

That night was the first of many where we would stay up late talking and laughing. Eventually, we migrated into his basement—away from his roommates' nosy eyes. Our friendship was beginning to transform into something more, something that neither one of us wanted to address . . . or stop.

I even talked about him with of my sorority sisters. Our subtle flirting had become increasingly public.

"You can't tell me that man doesn't want you." I rolled those words around in my mind, smiling. I had to admit—I was starting to want him too. But what did that mean? Was I really the type of girl to be with someone else's boyfriend? What about Smitty Stevie? Was any part of me doing this just to hurt him or prove a point?

I dismissed the thoughts and ignored the warnings about getting too close to Energetic Edward. We had never even kissed. He had a girlfriend and I had a situationship.

"We're just friends, girl. He has a girlfriend, remember?"

"Yeah…if that's what you want to call it."

Still, I noticed we were spending so much time together, I wondered when did he see his girlfriend? I justified it, and dismissed the claws of guilt trying to dig into my shoulders. We had done nothing more than hug and sit close on his futon. No kissing. *It's still very much platonic* was the lie I kept feeding myself.

Apparently, our chemistry was obvious to others. At a party one night, another one of my sorority sisters pulled me aside.

"Hey Carrie, are you still dating that one guy back home?"

I nodded, still snapping my fingers to the music.

"I thought so. That's what I told Josh when he asked if something was going on between you and E."

Cool as a cucumber, I asked, "Why would anyone think that?"

Though deep down, I knew. We gravitated toward each other wherever we were—locking eyes across the room. Making faces to make the other laugh or smile.

She laughed. "I said he was way too hyper for you. You're way more chill. He bounces around the room nonstop. He would annoy the mess outta me, so I know he would get on your nerves."

I bristled. She didn't know him like I did. Beneath the hyper energy was a calm, insightful, observant man who could read a room in seconds. He was intentional about making people feel welcome, loved bringing light to a space, and never let anyone stand alone. His energy was a gift, not an annoyance.

But I didn't say any of that. Instead, I gave her a dose of her own medicine about her own messy relationship.

"How are things going between you and Phillip? I heard ya'll fell out last week."

"Oh girl," she dismissed my question with a wave of her hand. "That is a story for another day. But let me get over there and say hi to my friend. You know she broke up with her boyfriend recently. Talk to you later!"

That night, I recapped the conversation to Energetic Edward, making him double over with laughter.

"I guess I need to stop being so flirty with you if people are starting to talk."

"I guess so," I said.

"But . . . I'm not sure if I want to."

This was the first time there was any mention of what was developing between us. And as much as I tried to deny it, I was starting to enjoy him as more than a friend.

To keep myself from falling for someone else's man, and to prove I wasn't "that girl", I gave Smitten Steven more of my attention. I called him in the mornings, returned missed calls more quickly, and tried to reconnect. But it didn't slow down my budding relationship with Energetic Edward. One night, we decided to hang out since we hadn't seen each other in a while. We did our normal routine of talking most of the night, but instead of him driving me back to campus, I stayed the night. I told myself it was innocent. We hadn't even kissed. *We're just friends.*

The level of denial I was feeding myself was Olympic-level. I was spending the night with someone else's boyfriend and then calling my pseudo-boyfriend in the morning.

(Side note: This is one of my reasons why I don't believe men and women can be "just friends." Strict boundaries are necessary, and in my experience it just never works. Fight me if you want to, but my experience speaks for itself.)

Eventually, our "innocent" nightly hang outs produced sweet kisses and soft touches. The line was crossed and lies began to follow.

We got strategic, calling our significant others first so there would be no question if we didn't answer. Then we would shut the world out and cocoon in our own bliss.

Sweet kisses became breathy moans, and the line wasn't just crossed—it was obliterated. I was now that girl. I could have turned away from her. I could have rejected the drama, the secrets, the inevitable fallout. But instead, I embraced her.

I was sneaky and sexy, lying and loving, deceiving and delightful all at the same time. What had I become? As a twenty-something, I was caught up and willing to ride things out, because I didn't have a solid plan B (B as in boyfriend) waiting on the sidelines.

For once, the Serial Dater didn't have a backup.

Chapter 5

When Moving for Love Becomes a Lesson in Letting Go

After graduating from college and stepping into the real world with my own apartment and a new (but boring) job, Energetic Edward and I finally made things official. He broke things off for good with his girlfriend, and I let go of my roster of random guys.

Once official, he became Entertaining Eddie.

We knew our relationship had a scandalous backstory, but we did our best to leave it in the past and focus on what could be. The long-distance relationship didn't faze us. We filled the gap with long nights on the phone, weekend road trips, and big, dreamy declarations about the future. "I love yous" rolled off our tongues as naturally as our ambitious plans. He was going to be a big name in entertainment. I was going to be the author-slash-corporate mogul. We would be the power couple of power couples. We picked our wedding song, imagined weekend drives up the coast, and even chose the name for our future daughter.

So, naturally when he eventually moved to Los Angeles, a year later … I followed. *(The things we do for love.)* Now, before you start thinking about us living happily ever after, I was in Los Angeles for two years before Entertaining Eddie and I called it quits.

Somewhere along the way, arguments started to outnumber the laughter. I was working an everyday job and figuring out how to be an adult in love. His focus was on chasing his dream career. I nagged him about getting a "real job" so we could do all the things we used to do back home. He pushed back, frustrated I didn't understand his artistic process or why a 9-to-5 wasn't part of his plan. He wanted me to understand his journey in discovering the road to success. I wanted him to sacrifice for me the way my dad sacrificed for my mom and sister—handle car repairs, take me out regularly, and pay for me to get my hair done. Looking back, I see that it was all about me. I wanted to make a husband out of my boyfriend without a ring, or even a clue of what being a wife truly meant.

One night, after a fight that lasted over several days, my phone rang.

"I think we need to break up."

My stomach dropped. Entertaining Eddie uttered the very words I didn't have the courage to say.

While I had anticipated this day and even thought about how I could end things, I wasn't prepared for the reality of it. The thought of life without Entertaining Eddie filled me with dread. I was scared to navigate such a big city as a single woman, thousands of miles away from my family and closest friends.

Fear slowly started to creep up my feet, curling upward, and wrapping its sharp tentacles around my legs.

As much as I hated to admit it, I cared about what people would think if I no longer had a boyfriend, especially after moving across the country to be with one. This thought only fueled my fear. It climbed higher, squeezing my stomach into knots whenever I replayed the part I played in our relationship unraveling. I wanted to embrace a new way of thinking but in short, swift movements, fear swirled around my body, pinning my arms down to my sides. Then, it coiled around my face, covering my eyes and mouth, whispering lies into my ears.

You're not pretty enough.

You're not talented enough to keep his attention.

He'll find someone better—and she'll benefit from all the effort you put in.

Eventually, fear seeped into my heart, where it found a cavernous hole—one that had been forming over the years of serial dating, and made itself at home.

I was scared to be alone.

The hole was small at first. I figured if Entertaining Eddie would just do more of what made me happy, it would close. I thought I could fill it with the satisfaction of a relationship and the security of the plans we'd made.

But the more I tried to fill it with the wrong things, the bigger it became. Sometimes the ache radiated physically, signaling my brain with sharp pangs that went deeper than heartbreak. It was a peculiar emptiness that gnawed at me, disrupted my sleep, and muddled my thoughts. At the time, I didn't recognize it for what it was. I thought it was heartbreak and hopelessness, dealing with a crushing blow to the dreams of marriage and kids I finally let myself imagine.

The truth is that the imagined future was heavily influenced by the nuptials happening all around me.

In my mid-late twenties, I saw a wave rising amongst some of my friends or acquaintances, one wedding after another. If a couple had been together since college or dating for more than two years, it was only a matter of time before I received a bridesmaid invitation. If I wasn't in the wedding, I would spend my extra funds traveling across the continent to attend them.

Part of the blame falls on the "be married before thirty" idea that somehow lodged itself into my brain.

In my mind, the plan looked like this:

Get married before thirty. Spend a couple years figuring each other out. Build successful careers. Make enough money to buy a house. Raise kids in said household—all before my eggs shriveled up.

And if that wasn't enough pressure, there was always the mind-numbing shock of a gynecologist casually dropping the phrase "freeze your eggs" during a mid-thirties annual appointment—just to make sure you left the office both informed and slightly panicked. *Ahem . . . but I digress.*

The hole in my heart kept growing— fed by false hopes of a future I'd never even submitted to God. I wanted what I wanted, but I'd never asked God what He wanted. Those false hopes mixed with the creeping dread that I might never meet someone who could make me feel the way I wanted to feel made the hole even deeper.

Instead of finding out why it was growing at the rate it was, Entertaining Eddie and I started playing a prolonged game of break-up to make up. It went something like this:

Bored? Call your ex.

Feeling nostalgic after talking with a friend who is loving married life? Call your ex.

Job promotion? Get your "oo-wee cookie"[1] from your ex.

Birthday plans? Invite your ex.

Had too much to drink? Drunk dial your ex.

Sad and not meeting anyone new? Hang out with your ex.

This was the story of my life for the next few years. Yep, years. (Even now, *I shake my head at the thought.*)

Yes, I went on dates and spent time with other men, but it was nothing more than a comparison game. They were my distractions. And in my immaturity, I clung to the broken philosophy: to get over one, you must get under another. The thing was, I was still getting under Entertaining Eddie from time to time while keeping everyone else at arm's length.

I knew I needed to heal. I knew I needed to walk away, but I craved familiarity. It was easier to run back to him than sit alone and deal with the distorted mess of my own feelings.

Entertaining Eddie was also seeing other people, and I knew it. I just chose to live in willful ignorance. Don't ask, don't tell became our unofficial policy.

But the thing about policies is that every few years they come up for renewal—or expiration.

And ours expired the day I got a call from my doctor's office.

---

[1] "oo-wee cookie" is a family term referring to getting acknowledged/kudos for any hard work or major accomplishment.

"Hi, Carrie. Can you come in as soon as possible? Dr. Preethi would like to discuss your pap smear results."

"What did the results say?" I asked, already feeling that slight irritation that came whenever a doctor's office sounded mysterious for no reason. If something was wrong, why couldn't they just tell me? Instead, they dangled this ominous *we need to talk* over my head.

"She would prefer to discuss this with you in person."

"I get that, but I have a really busy schedule today. Can you at least give me a hint, so I know what to expect?"

She sighed then said, "Your pap smear results came back with abnormal cells on your cervix. It's important that you speak with the doctor."

There was a sinking feeling in my stomach; the kind that robs you of your appetite and makes you feel like you need to throw up and use the bathroom at the same time.

"OK. When is the soonest I can come in?"

"Today we just had an opening at 1:30. You'll be the first patient when she returns from lunch."

"I'll take it."

As I drove to the doctor's office, I considered calling my parents to ask for prayer but decided against it. I didn't want them to worry, and I didn't even know what abnormal cells on my cervix actually meant.

When I arrived, I was led to my ob-gyn's office instead of an exam room. Her desk was a mess—papers stacked haphazardly—and the only personal touch was a single photo of a dog and a little girl with brown pigtails and a gap-toothed smile.

"Hi, Carrie," she said, pronouncing it care-ray in an accent that I couldn't quite place. "Thanks for coming in so soon. I want to discuss your pap smear results. They came back abnormal and positive for the human papillomavirus, also known as HPV. Have you heard of it before?"

I nodded. Of course, I had. But never in a way that I thought would apply to me.

"It is a sexually transmitted infection that is very common. Most times, younger sexually active individuals get it and it goes away on its own. But for women in your age group, it can also cause cervical cancer when not properly treated. With proper screening and tests, we can help prevent cervical cancer. I am going to recommend you see a colleague of mine who specializes in female care and can give you more information since your test showed abnormal cells on your cervix. He will probably recommend a LEEP procedure."

"Could there have been a test or something to prevent this?" I asked.

"There are vaccines now, but you would have had to take that prior to you becoming sexually active."

"Are there tests that show if my partner has it?"

"If it were a male carrier, no. There are no ways to screen for it unless he has symptoms like genital warts."

After that, I only caught about sixty percent of what she said because there was a pulsing sensation between my ears. My thoughts collapsed into a single sentence: *I have an STI.* Words like "vaccine" and "age group" floated past like debris in murky water.

I snapped back and realized she was handing me a brochure to discuss STIs and a referral slip for her colleague.

I don't remember if I said thank you, or even how I made it out to my car. I sat there shaking, blasting the air conditioning.

A fountain of tears threatened to flow down my cheeks. I took deep gulps of air. Driving home was not an option.

I needed someone to translate medical jargon into plain English.

I dialed my best friend who was in residency to become a gynecologist.

As soon as she answered, the words tumbled out between sobs. She listened, excusing herself from wherever she was, and let me unload every mispronounced medical term, every panicked thought.

She said the same things the doctor had said—that it was common, and "just about everybody" gets it.

"I'm not everybody," I sobbed. "I'm not out here wilding out. Entertaining Eddie is the only person I've been sleeping with."

"True, but are you the only person he's sleeping with?"

Silence.

Deep down, I knew the answer.

I'd seen it in the way he kissed differently, the way he shielded his phone when I was near, the way his presence thinned out until he felt half-there. I had the evidence, but I chose the blinders. It was easier than facing life without him.

He had become such a staple in my life, as inconsistent and unhealthy as it was, at least he was there. At the time, I told myself that it was better than nothing. Better than starting over. Better than risking disappointment with someone new.

"Have you talked to him yet?" she asked.

"No. I don't know what to say." I lied. I knew what I wanted to say. I wanted to blame him for endangering me. I wanted to cry my eyes out from the betrayal and guilt. I wanted to call him everything in the book and hear him take responsibility, so

I wouldn't have to. I wanted to tell him how terrified I was of having an STI that could cause cancer and beg him to fix it so we wouldn't have to end things for good.

My despair transformed into panic. Panic that this was the reason, or the excuse to leave him. Panic that I'd lose the one person I'd convinced myself I couldn't live without.

I idolized the idea of us—the future we'd planned, the empty promises, the fantasy of marriage, more than I valued my own peace. And now, I didn't know where to go from here. "Well, you need to tell him." Her voice shifted into doctor mode. She explained the procedure, the next steps, the statistics.

What she didn't address was the condemnation clawing at me. The shame of knowing I'd ignored my gut. The weight of realizing I had chosen this by staying, by settling, and by letting my desires outweigh my wisdom. I knew HPV was common, but was it common to stay in a situationship that could have been prevented? I berated myself. Had I been strong enough to leave a situation that was emotionally unhealthy, I would not be in this place.

"Are you still there?"

"I'm here," I whispered.

"It's not as bad as it sounds. You'll get through this." She reassured me. And I believed her that, physically, yes, I would certainly get through this. But emotionally? I knew the road would be jagged.

Because it wasn't the diagnosis that haunted me. It was the regret. The shame. The knowing better, and still doing it anyway.

I hung up, knowing that things needed to change. I had let my sexual desires endanger me, cloud my judgment, and strip me bare of the emotional boundaries I thought I had.

Enter Hope.

Dear ~~Diary~~ . . . Dear God,

I feel like I should be writing, "Are you there, God? It's me, Margaret." It has been so long since I've taken the time to talk to you.

I'm sorry.

I feel like such a cliché—running to you only because my heart was crushed and I found myself desperate.

I'm sorry, so sorry that I didn't follow your instructions or pay attention to the promptings you have been stirring on the inside of me.

I can't believe I let this whole back-and-forth thing bring me to this place.

And now, I've got an STI, one that could cause cervical cancer. I know it's my fault.

I'm not sure how my life has come to this, but I am sure I need your help. Please heal me and help me make better decisions.

Your daughter.

Chapter 6

No Sex, No Problem . . . Right?

The word *hope* is tattooed on the outside of my right wrist. Some people buy trinkets or book trips to memorialize milestones. I decided to tattoo mine because it was hope that led me back to Jesus Christ. Hope that there was more to life than my broken heart.

It sparked when I was grieving the death of my relationship. Entertaining Eddie and I had envisioned our future in vivid detail, including waking up on sunny Saturday mornings in LA and driving down the coast. With that dream gone, and a past full of questionable choices and constant discontentment, I found myself back in the pew of my childhood church. There, I remembered the gentle way God had first called me to Himself. How His peace had wrapped around me like a soft blanket. I longed for that peace again.

Joy, however, felt like it had taken off in a sprint in the opposite direction, putting miles between us. No job promotion, no romantic pursuit, no friendship, no drunken night out, no new hair weave, no new outfit or pair of shoes could remedy the ache. I was thirsty for a well that never runs dry, but kept sipping from empty cups.

After a very new promotion or career change, I hoped the newness or change would quench the thirst and fill the hole that was growing deeper. I kept running up my credit card bill because it was easier to buy a false sense of fancy than sit alone with my feelings. I didn't want to face the healing I needed. It was easier to run to the mall, order dinner and dessert then pretend I was satisfied—rather than seek the One who is joy Himself.

But little did I know, hope was stirring and was just a bookstore visit away.

I can't remember which bookstore I wandered into or what made me stop in that aisle. But I do remember the cover that caught my eye: the word *Hope* written boldly across the front. The book was *The One Year Book of Hope* by Nancy Guthrie—a fifty-two-week devotional about how the love of Jesus Christ can heal the wounds of disappointment and bring hope for when life hurts the most. Gutherie had lost two children due to a rare disease called Zellweger Syndrome. One of them, a baby girl, was named Hope.

At night, I would curl up in my bed and cradle that book in my hands. From the very first page, Guthrie acknowledged how the book was for anyone who is grieving. My grief paled in comparison to losing a child, but I had to admit to myself that I was indeed grieving— grieving the loss of a life I thought I'd have.

Living as a single woman with no real direction in my late twenties wasn't the story I'd pictured. I felt like a forever bridesmaid, spending money I didn't have to plan bachelorette weekends and send baby shower gifts across the country.

I needed healing.

Although I still attended church here and there, my heart craved an intimate relationship with Jesus. Gutherie's words pointed me back to Scripture. Each week, her reflections seemed to speak directly to where my heart and head were—as if she could see my thoughts and feelings. Each devotional was anchored in Bible verses I could study, meditate on, and let sink into the empty places of my soul.

The Bible came alive in a new way. Not as a rulebook or a Sunday habit, but as a lifeline. A love letter. A well that would never run dry.

In preparation for sharing this part of my story, I pulled *The One Year Book of Hope* off my shelf and opened to the dog-eared pages stained with my tears. Some were tears of sadness, but many were tears of repentance and reconciliation.

I remembered reading the scriptures she referenced and how they led me to devour biblical stories I once heard as a child, but now with fresh eyes that had lived some life. Abraham's journey from his father's land to the land that God promised. Joseph, the dreamer, was sold into slavery and thrown into a pit, yet was raised to the palace. The same passages that once felt like distant Sunday School tales now pulsed with relevance.

I didn't realize it then, but God was speaking into my life from every direction. I'd study that week's devotional, and then the Sunday sermon would align perfectly. In between devotionals, I'd come home from work, sit in my oversized chair with my legs dangling over the side and read my Bible or listen to Joyce Meyer sermons. My life wasn't exciting, but it was peaceful. It was the most peace I'd felt in years. The constant strife that had been my normal began to dissolve.

In those quiet nights in my apartment, God was reshaping my heart. Through His Word, through biblical teachings from my pastor, and through voices like Joyce Meyer, He revealed His loving character to me again. I began to grasp what grace really meant—that my mistakes didn't define how He sees me. God had forgiven me, and now, He was inviting me to forgive myself.

As I studied Paul's writings in the New Testament, God, in His loving way, began convicting me to honor His commandments and value my body over what any man could offer. He was teaching me to live as someone who is truly fearfully and wonderfully made, to love Him first, and to see myself through His unfailing love.

Little by little, I began unlearning much of what I thought it meant to live for Jesus. I abandoned the man-made traditions of religion from my childhood—marked by preachers thundering about fire and brimstone—and stepped into truly knowing Him as my Comforter, my Redeemer, and my King.

I began to see that Jesus didn't give us a list of dos and don'ts to keep us from joy or fun. His boundaries are a gift—protecting me from a broken view of love, from carrying unnecessary burdens, and from living enslaved to sins I was never meant to live with. In His Word, I discovered the beauty of staying close to Him. And I saw with new clarity that apart from Him, I would only find myself back in those same familiar places of hurt and brokenness.

But while my heart was changing, my habits still had some catching up to do. I wish that I could tell you that after those beautiful encounters with Jesus in my apartment every night, studying my Bible and living peacefully in my solitude, my dedication deepened, I made a vow of abstinence, and I never gave in to temptation.

Um . . . nah.

As I started living for Jesus again, I had to face my serial dater days and examine my view of relationships—especially sexual ones. Jesus began showing me how sexual experiences had shaped me and my relationships with men. I never had a true understanding of sex.

My "sex talk" as a child could be summed up in one sentence: "You have sex, you get pregnant." And like many churches, the only teaching I heard was don't have sex before marriage because it's a sin, or you might get pregnant.

That's not enough for a hormone-driven young adult who is being inundated with sexual content at every turn. Nobody explained the emotional and spiritual impact of letting someone into my body, my personal, mental, and emotional space. Instead, I was shamed or hit over the head with fear and threats of hell. Nobody talked about the confusion of being with one person while thinking about another ... or comparing them. No one told me how hard it would be to walk away from someone who is unhealthy once we had been intimate for years, or about the emptiness that followed when I kept giving my goodies to people who didn't deserve them.

What I needed was someone to explain how sex is a God-ordained gift meant for marriage, not just to keep me "out of trouble" but to protect my heart. Experiencing it outside of covenant doesn't just risk pregnancy—it will entangle your soul, cloud your judgement, and have you doing ignorant, irrational things for the wrong person.

Simply telling me not to sin, warning me about pregnancy, and layering on the church-shame (*only on the girl, mind you*) were not what I needed to hear. I needed to understand how sex outside of covenant could shape my future. I needed someone to break down that sex isn't just physical—it's a joining together, a spiritual connection. And when you're joined to someone in that way, the connection doesn't disappear just because they leave or the relationship ends.

At the time, I didn't have examples of inspiring, young, fly women who were living by God's standards and willing to talk about living pure. I knew about people sneaking around, getting caught only when a pregnancy became visible. Even then, no one shared what they learned or why they made the decisions they did.

So my ideas about sex were formed from 90s R&B music—just like kids today are learning it from explicit hip hop lyrics, reality television, and social media's glorification of sexual exploration.

But culture cannot define what God created.

I turned to scripture to learn God's view on relationships. I heard Joyce Meyer say that studying Jesus' behavior would reveal His character, so I dove into the gospels of Matthew, Mark, Luke, and John. There I discovered His fairness, His duality of being fully God and fully human, His unconventional ways of reaching people, His use of symbolism, His disregard for timing, His inability to sin, His dedication, and above all, His truth.

Jesus was spitting fire when He said, "The Spirit is willing but the flesh is weak" (Matt 26:41). My spirit was willing to live wholeheartedly for Him, but my flesh? My flesh was out here like, *wait—no cussing, no wild partying, and no sex? What are you doing to me?*

When you commit to living for God, the enemy will creep in—especially in the area you are most reluctant to surrender. For me, that was sex. I vowed not to have sexual intercourse before marriage ... but I left other things "on the table." In my mind, I could be holy while still doing some things without doing *the* thing.

Let me make it plain: I wanted sexual closeness without the "guilt" of crossing *that* line. At first, it felt like a win. I'd leave an encounter feeling proud—telling myself I'd accomplished something because I hadn't gone "all the way." *I'm doing better than I used to.* But Jesus, in His merciful way, pricked my conscience and convicted me. It was as if He whispered, "And does this make you feel any better?"

No.

I was still left with the same emptiness. Sharing my body in a way that no longer honored my Heavenly Father. It wasn't just about me or the other person anymore. I had invited Jesus into my heart, and the Word I was devouring was now rising up—making it impossible to be comfortable with the behaviors He was healing me from.

I ignored the conviction at first. It was easier to listen to my flesh when it came to physical gratification. But ignoring what God imprints on my heart has never worked long-term. Playing with fire and expecting not to get burned is not realistic. Inch by inch, I crept closer to the line until I eventually crossed it.

After sleeping with a guy, I remember slipping into the bathroom and burying my face in a towel, trying to muffle the sounds of my sobs. I was mad at myself for letting it get to this point, not heeding God's warning and listening to what my body wanted instead of what I knew was best for me.

The truth was, I also hadn't fully surrendered this part of my life to God. MY "boundaries" weren't really about honoring Him—they were about protecting myself. Not having sex was my way of controlling the risk of heartbreak. I knew that if I crossed that line, I would be tethered to them and could risk making clouded decisions that could wreak havoc on other areas of my life. I didn't want to be "stupid for love" *again*.

So I built walls. Every interaction stayed surface-level. No deep vulnerability. No real intimacy. My self-protection was my defense mechanism—and my downfall. Because when your motives are about you instead of Him, you're left trying to fight in your own strength.

I imagine Jesus shaking His head with a smile, thinking, "My dear one, you think you're going to be able to do this dating without sex thing without Me?"

I tried. And failed miserably... more than once. Each time, I found myself in the same place— of wanting more but settling for less. I wanted a relationship but settled for seasonal cuddles. I was trying to create my own guidelines versus following the ones Christ had given me.

Doing it without the Holy Spirit was futile. There is a reason He is called our Helper. God knew there would be things we are not designed to do alone.

I hadn't yet reached the place where I took everything before God and laid it at his feet. But if I was going to honor God with all of me—mind, soul, body, and spirit—the Holy Spirit was going to have to step in.

Dating with sex off the table was uncharted territory. I didn't have role models to show me what it looked like, but I had a heart that wanted to honor God.

This was going to be a ride. And I was buckled up—ready to go.

Dear Father,

I love you. Thank you for your mercy as you have opened my eyes to the truth of sex and how I react to it. I can't unsee it or unlearn it. However, I need your help in living this thing out. Holy Spirit, when temptation comes, rise up in me and remind me whose I am. I am above and not beneath. I am a child of God and an heir to the throne. You have fashioned me for a purpose, and my feelings don't dictate my actions. Sex is not the whole purpose of a relationship, and I can survive without it. I just haven't for so long.

Forgive me, Lord. I repent for letting my fleshly desires lead me instead of you.

But this . . . this is uncharted territory, Lord. I've obviously been doing it the wrong way and seeking loopholes to do what I want to do versus what You would have me to do. I want the words of my mouth and the meditations of my heart to be pleasing to you.

Um, Lord—I'm gonna need directions for how to do this. It feels like I'm lessening my pool of eligible men even more by taking sex off the table. Who is going to date me when we can't have sex? And how do I just not do it?

I surrender my need to control the situation and ask that you control it instead.

Really yours this time,
Carrie Lea

Chapter 7

When God Says Not Yet

Career progression took me up the California coast to the Bay Area. With Christ's love now filling the gaping hole in my heart, I felt ready to dip my toe back into the dating waters. I had a renewed outlook and wanted to see what life could look like when I walked in faith and obedience.

A new city meant endless possibilities. Each neighborhood had its own quirks, and I found real joy in exploring shopping centers, cozy cafes, and hidden gems of restaurants.

New surroundings also meant new friends and new hangout spots. I met Sunny, another young woman walking a similar path of living for Christ. We both wanted a place where we could mix, mingle, and meet new people. There is a certain awkwardness to making friends as an adult—you're syncing up schedules, gauging personalities, and wondering if your new friend is the type to flip tables or just sit in awkward silence.

Thankfully, Sunny was the perfect middle ground. We laughed easily, conversation flowed, and I felt the freedom to be my authentic self, sprinkling in the occasional inappropriate comment. (*God was still working on my mouth.*)

We found a cool spot in a hip, thriving part of town. By day, it was a restaurant. But as the skies darkened, the music cranked up a bit louder and soon there was more looking, talking, and drinking than eating.

The vibrant interior matched the energy from the crowd—large plush couches with low tables, a big bar anchoring the center, and cream-colored chandeliers casting a warm glow. Two large marble pillars framed a floor-to-ceiling glass display of liquor and wine, giving the place a sleek, polished feel.

Men and women were shoulder to shoulder at the bar with big smiles and squinted eyes, which let me know the liquor was flowing and so was the conversation.

I saw twists, afros, locs, curly tendrils, bone straight inches, and low-cut Caesars with the deep waves from most of the men and women. It was a sea of tall, short, stocky, and cocky—each one trying (and failing) to play it cool while stealing glances at the competition.

Sunny and I did a couple of laps around the bar before snagging a couch seat. We weren't there long before men sauntered over to start a conversation. One asked what I liked to do for fun, while another tried to send a drink my way.

This is what I call a "Meat Market." Everyone was on the market, everyone was shopping. Some were prime cuts fetching top bids, others . . . let's just say, priced to move. Whether you preferred your meat lean and trim or a full beefsteak indulgence, the options were there. Everyone was hungry. And everyone was hunting.

We did our fair share of smiling and declining while chatting about our expectations of the night, upcoming plans, and other things we might explore.

Sunny and I were both hyper-aware that what we thought would be a casual, cute night out had morphed into an evening at a club-slash-lounge. I wasn't sure how I felt about it. I had just left this kind of environment in my previous city, and part of me wondered if this is where the new, more grown-up version of me who loved Jesus should be hanging out. Still, we decided to stick it out. And if I'm being honest, the attention was … nice.

The bathroom line confirmed my suspicions: yes, this was definitely a club. It was long enough to make you reconsider your water intake, and the women in line were unusually friendly—like "I'll hold your purse while you go" friendly. When I came out, a man was leaning casually against the wall by the corner to go back to the main area. He resembled a chocolate milk-dud wearing silver-framed sunglasses. Yes—sunglasses. At night. Inside. That should have been my first indicator to keep walking.

"Excuse me," he said, grabbing my elbow (*reason number two I should have kept walking*), "Can I talk to you for a minute?" I had zero desire to get caught up in conversation, but instead of saying "thank you" and moving on, I stood there smiling while he told me how beautiful he thought I was.

I couldn't tell you everything he said after complimenting my looks. I was too busy plotting my escape without resorting to a lie. I did not want to give him my contact information, yet there I was—still standing there. I'd like to "blame it on the goose," but I was sober and very much in my right mind.

Then it happened. Mid-sentence, he let out a slight burp, and the smell of garlic and cognac assaulted my senses. You could almost see the green fumes floating in the air between us. I tried not to gag.

"Excuse me," he said quickly, waving a hand in front of his mouth like that would erase what just happened.

That was my cue. I politely excused myself and made my way back towards Sunny—only to find someone else sitting in my seat. I raised my eyebrows as I approached, silently asking if she needed rescuing or if she was enjoying herself. Her smile and easy laughter told me to slow my roll.

So I stood back, scanning the room for this new vantage point. That's when I saw him. My gaze caught his bright smile, circled the room, and found its way back to him.

He had a head full of slightly unruly, coily hair and a casual confidence that drew me in. Dark-rimmed glasses. Pale pink button-up shirt—untucked—paired with dark-wash jeans and sneakers. The shirt's color made his deep complexion look even richer. Lean, runner's build. A glass of white wine in hand. And that smile… it didn't just catch my attention, it kept it.

He walked up to me and said, "I've been waiting in line all night to talk with you."

"Lucky you," I flashed my best flirtatious smile. "Now's your time."

"Oh-ho-ho, she's beautiful *and* she's cocky," he laughed.

"No, I'm just teasing," I lied. I was cocky.

His name was Academic Aaron, and apparently, he had been watching Sunny and me catch attention all night.

"So, you've been stalking me?" I asked with a wink. *Who was I?* Winking, smiling, and holding a conversation with a cute guy? Normally, I saw someone attractive and diverted my eyes or mumbled something corny.

"Not at all. Just observing. There's something about you." His gaze dropped briefly a sec. "And I'm not the only one who sees it."

I shrugged. "Beauty can only do so much. It's a meat market in here, and most of these guys have one goal in mind."

"Is that the kind of game you've received tonight? Let me get you a drink so you can tell me more about it." He glanced toward Sunny, now alone and raising her eyebrows at me. "Is that champagne?"

"No, sparkling water, with a lime, please."

He feigned shock. "No one's gotten you a real drink tonight?"

I tilted my head and smiled. "I'm not drinking, so no."

He stood there for a moment, looking at me longer than felt comfortable. I glanced around, wondering if he'd heard me. "Why aren't you drinking?"

"That's an odd question," I replied. "I just saved you some money, and you're now asking me why?"

"It's not often that I meet someone who doesn't drink."

Before moving to the Bay Area, I'd decided to give alcohol a break. I didn't want it to cloud my judgment as I adjusted to a new city and new friendships.

"Well, I am one of a kind," I replied.

He chuckled. "So I'm learning. Your complexion is exquisite."

"Thank you. It was a gift. Looks like you received it too."

"I did but it doesn't shimmer like yours." He obviously wasn't new to this flirting game. Thankfully, I wasn't getting sleaze-bucket vibes, just genuine interest. And I was into it.

"Eh, it's just Vaseline." We both laughed.

"What kind of work do you do?" he asked. I told him about my recent transition into a corporate role for a major retailer.

"Congratulations! That's awesome."

"Thanks. I'm pretty proud of this next step. What do you do?"

"I'm a musician."

I paused. Not because I had anything against musicians, but after Entertaining Eddie, I was wary of meeting another artist or attracting the dreamers of the world.

He caught my hesitation. "I should probably add that yes, I do work a regular job, but singing and writing music are my passion. I'm a man of the arts."

I smiled and felt myself relax a bit.

We volleyed playful banter for a few more minutes, each of us noticing how easy the conversation flowed. He seemed to enjoy my wit, and I liked how quick he was with his comebacks.

I told him I needed to get back to my friend, not wanting to be rude.

"Well, I have thoroughly enjoyed talking to you, he said. "I would love to continue the conversation."

For the first time in a long time, I felt a spark of excitement. In the world of singledom, you meet plenty of people, especially in spots like this where the drinks were flowing and the vibe was flirtatious. But I learned the hard way that just because a guy asks for your number doesn't mean you'll actually talk. Sometimes, once the liquid courage wears off, he can't even remember your name—or he suddenly recalls he has a girlfriend and had no business asking for your number in the first place.

But Academic Aaron seemed different. We exchanged numbers, and he emphasized that while he would send a text to ensure I had his number, he was more of a phone guy and would give me a call that week.

I nodded, said goodnight, and made my way back to Sunny. We left soon after, promising to meet up again soon.

True to his word, Academic Aaron texted me a few days later to confirm a time to talk. This was off to a good start, and I looked forward to talking with him.

Once on the phone, we breezed through the small talk and went a little deeper. He mentioned he was a few years older than me and wanted to be upfront about it. He also said he believed in making his intentions clear and wasn't into playing games.

Academic Aaron couldn't see it, but I was giving vigorous head nods. I liked a man who made his intentions known from the get-go.

Then he dropped the next piece of information: he had a three-month-old son. He "got caught up" (his words, not mine) with his now baby mama but realized he didn't want a long-term relationship with her. She had just moved to Las Vegas, and he was still figuring out how to be present in his son's life. Pause.

A man with a child wasn't a deal-breaker. When dating over thirty, it's more common than not. However, a newborn child was different. Newborns came with a unique set of demands. The mother was usually still a major factor—often with lingering feelings involved. And the level of intimacy required between the parents to raise the child well meant that anybody new to the situation would have to take a back seat. If he were an involved father, the baby would come first, as it should.

I was very anti-kids at that time. I preferred to be prioritized and didn't want to share affections or plans with someone's child. I knew that about myself, and with that in mind, I had no real interest in exploring anything further with Academic Aaron.

Still, not wanting to appear rude or abrupt, I asked, "How are you managing that?"

He launched into a long dissertation about the importance of accountability and making the best of the situation. He was honest about his communication with his son's mother and where their relationship stood.

Then, he changed the subject by asking what I like to do when I'm not working. I explained that, outside of random nights like the one we met, my life was mostly work, gym, eating, and church.

He guffawed. "I had a degree in church until I opened my eyes and realized that I was being deceived."

His tone shifted—condescending, almost smug. He went on to describe being raised in church, fed what he called the "lies" of Christianity, and watching hypocrites deceive the rest of the world. He'd grown up Apostolic, believing in Jesus, but after reading, studying, and acquiring "knowledge," he now knew the truth.

This was a turn I did not see coming.

I was still new to this whole Christian dating thing, but I knew that dating someone of a different faith was not an option. Part of my vow to let Jesus handle my love story was because I didn't know how to date as a Christian woman and needed His help. I knew that dating as a Christian meant that we did things differently. Someone of another faith wouldn't understand that, and in Academic Aaron's case, wouldn't respect it either. I was beginning to know Jesus personally, and this was not an area I was willing to compromise on. His view on Christianity was the final nail in the "this is not for me" coffin.

I tried to politely end the conversation without giving a specific reason beyond, "I think we just don't see eye-to-eye on some things." But Academic Aaron wasn't going to let it go that easily.

"What? You won't be unequally yoked with a non-believer?" He asked in a mocking tone. "You're believing that whole story."

I could practically hear his eyes rolling through the phone.

I explained it wasn't just about the verse where Paul warned against being unequally yoked. I told him I wanted a marriage where my husband and I could pray together, worship together, and connect spiritually. I didn't want anything—or anyone—that could pull me away from Christ. I knew he and I weren't anywhere close to marriage, but I wasn't dating just to date. Been there, done that. I was looking for something lasting, and that wasn't possible with someone who denied God and rejected Christ. "I'll go to church with you," he offered. "I'll even pray with you. I'm just saying that I don't believe the same thing." He went on about how his academic knowledge had "opened his eyes," insisting Jesus isn't who I think He is. He ridiculed my faith, calling me close-minded and archaic.

The more he talked, the more I just wanted to get off the phone.

When he finally tired of hearing himself speak, he asked, "Are you really willing to throw this away and not even see where this could go, all because of what you believe? I know you feel the chemistry here. It was undeniable the night we met. That's why I was so drawn to you."

"It's not just that." I really didn't want to waste more time explaining. By now, we'd been on the phone for over an hour. I was spent.

"What? It's my son, isn't it? I knew you would have an issue because you got real quiet as soon as I mentioned that situation."

He had no clue. My silence wasn't about his son—it was because the equation had become crystal clear:

Aspiring artist role (been there, suffered through that) + the high probability for baby-momma-drama with a newborn son (seen the movie and read that book) + the self-righteous pride fueling his monologue (currently living that) = future disaster.

The math was mathing. The disjointed faith was the square of the equation.

Unwilling to feed into his antics and reasonings, I gave him a simple, "This just wouldn't work. Take care," and hung up the phone.

I sat there a bit befuddled. Things went south so quickly. As inexperienced as I was in non-monogamous dating, I wasn't sure what to make of it. Discouragement and defeat began to creep in. Would I ever meet a guy where the chemistry was mutual, the banter came easy, and he had a relationship with God? Was that too much to ask?

Curled up in my oversized chair, phone in my lap, I felt vulnerable, exposed … and doubtful.

That's when I heard God say, "Not yet."

It was so clear and distinct, I looked around the room to see if my TV was on or where the voice could have come from. I quickly realized that God had spoken into my spirit. There was no denying it.

I'd always heard church folks say things like, "God told me" or "God spoke to me," but I never understood how they knew. If it wasn't an audible voice, how could you be sure?

Once, I asked my father what it sounds like when God speaks. He explained that God often uses a tone or voice familiar to you. It will often sound like your own voice but there's a knowing deep within. Some people call it a gut feeling, but it's greater than that.

He went on to explain that when you accept Christ as your Lord and Savior, you invite the Holy Spirit to live within you. The Holy Spirit is our Helper and Comforter, guiding us in what we should or shouldn't do. That inner voice will feel familiar, but it won't cater to your flesh. In fact, it will often nudge you to do the opposite of what your flesh wants because our flesh wants what glorifies us, not God.

My sister added to this truth by sharing that the enemy is not going to encourage you. He's not going to speak from a place of grace and love like the Holy Spirit does. His goal is to steal, kill, and destroy. The Spirit's goal is to love, correct, and guide you back to the Lord.

I knew it was God because the disappointment and discouragement that had been creeping in were suddenly gone. In their place was peace … and contentment. Instead of replaying the "what-ifs" about a man who clearly wasn't the one, I felt indifferent. I knew I was on the path God had for my life. I hadn't compromised my faith for the sake of a date. And I hadn't moved forward with someone just to avoid being alone.

I was in a new city. I was going to be physically alone at times. Those were just facts. Thankfully, I'd already learned to entertain myself when I first moved to California.

Before I even arrived in Los Angeles, I told Entertaining Eddie that I wasn't going to rely on him for a social life. I'd make my own friends, explore the city on my own, and discover what it had to offer. I didn't want my world outside of work to revolve around him, especially if we broke up.

So I made a point to go out to eat alone, try new coffee shops, listen to live music, and watch movies by myself. Exploring the city without someone else and enjoying my own company became my way of establishing independence and individuality. I carried that same mentality into the Bay Area. While I had one close friend there, I was intentional about not relying on her and her family. I needed to know who I was apart from anyone else.

Dating was no different.

I was determined to let God lead, and if that meant telling them I couldn't pursue anything because of our different faiths, so be it.

It wasn't lost on me that as soon as I got serious about my faith and committed to dating God's way, temptation showed up dressed as opportunity. The last thing the enemy wants is obedience to God. He doesn't mind if we go to church or even if we read our Bible. What rattles him is when we start applying what we learn and God begins to change our nature. That's when he gets irritated and tries to derail us. The devil is not creative, but that sucker sure is persistent.

Not long after that, my pastor taught from Joshua 1:9, when Joshua steps into leadership and prepares to lead the Israelites into the Promised Land. One of his points discussed the strength it takes to live counter-culturally. When everyone else seems to be getting the very thing you long for and doing it in the way that you know isn't God's best, it takes courage to stand firm. Relying on your own strength will only get you so far; you have to rely on the Holy Spirit to keep you steady. My pastor spoke about the courage it takes to walk in faith, to take God at his word and refuse compromise. The boundaries God gives us in Scripture aren't there to keep us from joy—they are there to protect us from the harm we can't yet see. This was confirmation that I had done the right thing by ending the conversation with Academic Aaron before it ever had the chance to turn into something more.

Hearing God's "Not Yet" has been an anchor in lonely seasons when I've wondered if I'd been forgotten. "Not yet" isn't no. I've heard His "No" before—clear, final, and undeniable. But I believe this "Not Yet" was His way of showing me that He wants to reveal Himself in my life first. God's hope never leads to disappointment.

Still ... there's a space between *not yet* and yes.

Hi Lord,

Thank you for being a God of wisdom and discernment.

What are your thoughts on online dating? It's a topic not directly discussed in the Bible, but it kinda feels like a Sarah and Hagar moment. Is online dating just me trying to make a relationship happen for myself? I've seen it work for others, but it feels like I'm trying to help you (as if you need my help for anything).

I dunno. Let me know what you think.

Amen.

Chapter 8

Online Dating: Proof God Has a Sense of Humor

"You need to put yourself out there," a married woman told me, putting extra emphasis on *need*.

I resisted the urge to put extra emphasis on rolling my eyes.

Why is there this assumption that single people are just sitting at home, twiddling their thumbs, binge-watching Netflix, and still expecting Mr. or Mrs. Right to knock on their front door? Granted, the pandemic made the sitting-at-home part way more common, and while that kind of meet-cute would be lovely—most of us realize a spouse isn't going to magically appear in our living room.

Now, my God is able to do exceedingly and abundantly above all I could dare ask or think, but I even I knew I had to leave the house to be seen. Either that or keep ordering items online and pray the most handsome delivery driver showed up at my door and was instantly attracted to my stay-at-home-looking-like-a-slob fashion (*I'd given this some thought*). Possible? Yes. Likely? No.

So when I heard the advice, *put yourself out there*, my first response was, "What does that even mean?" Where is this elusive 'there' that everyone refers to? Can I put it into my GPS to try to beat the estimated arrival time?

I assume that these well-meaning (and usually married) folks were referring to "there" as the dating scene. A scene that had transformed drastically since their dating days. Half of them met in college or before social media was even a thought, yet they still find it helpful to offer advice as if they have any idea what it is like to date now.

Take online dating apps, for example. They're the primary source for most people trying to meet someone today. But to me, they felt vain, unrealistic, and impersonal. Let's also not leave out unexpectedly humbling.

In the Christian dating world, online apps can be a bit taboo. Some believe it's forcing the hand of God and going against the scripture that says, "Whosoever findeth a wife, findeth a good thing and obtaineth favor of the Lord. (*Yes, I went King James version on y'all.*) And I don't disagree. But I also believe God works however He wants to work. For some, online dating can be the tool He uses. For others, it's a hard pass.

When I chose to join the millions of others in the online dating experience, I had to check my motives—my heart condition, if you will. Some Christians jump on the apps because they are tired of waiting on God and want to control the outcome. Their timeline isn't matching up, so they take matters into their own hands. Then when they meet said new boo, they slap a "God did it" label on it, while God is really standing off the side and saying, "Nah, that wasn't me."

Other Christians, meanwhile, look at how the world dates and want a taste of that experience. They want to be out in the scene, meeting people who feed their ego and help them avoid the real issue of why they can't be alone. Being with someone feels easier than being single, because being alone means addressing what's really going on in the heart. It means asking why that last relationship didn't last, or why it feels safer to run into someone else's arms rather than the arms of the One who gives ultimate comfort.

For some, online dating becomes an endless cycle of partners that feed the ego while distracting from deeper issues. These cycles often mask childhood wounds—wounds God longs to uncover so they don't follow us into marriage, impact our children, or ripple into future generations.

(But ahem . . . everybody ain't ready for that conversation.)

Yet I also believe online dating can be an act of faith. Not everyone uses it to control outcomes. Some step onto the apps with open hands, not dictating the how, but creating space where God can do His best work. God doesn't need our help, but He honors our submissiveness and willingness to partner with Him. Books don't write themselves. Paychecks don't appear without effort. Relationships aren't maintained by just one person.

When I first ventured into the world of online dating, I leaned into the act-of-faith posture. I didn't jump in blindly or out of frustration. I prayed first, listened, and when I didn't sense a "no," I moved forward with discernment.

Truth be told, the first time I signed up (yes, I've willingly subjected myself to this peculiar torture more than once), it was to partly prove a point. I wanted to silence the well-meaning but incredulous comments telling me to "put myself out there." So, I did.

I chose the site that had a reputation for being serious—the one people used when they were actually looking for a spouse, not just a situationship. It was pricier than the others, but it boasted more success stories. A few of my co-workers had met their lifelong mates on this site as well.

Of course, for every success story they shared, they also had a handful of horror stories and specific strategies. One kept a full spreadsheet tracking every date—where they went, what she wore, and her overall rating of the date. Another stored notes in her phone just to keep each suitor straight.

As a Black woman living in the Bay Area who wanted to date a Christian man and wasn't having sex before marriage, I was pretty sure I wouldn't need a spreadsheet. Those two requirements alone narrowed my dating pool to a kiddie-sized pond.

Still, my coworkers were kind enough to help me set up my profile. And believe me, profile-building is not a one-person job. I wanted to come across as authentic but not too vulnerable, interesting but not elusive, funny but not cheeky. Since I communicate much better in person than over a screen, my goal was simple: spark enough interest to get from messages to an actual conversation, and eventually, to a date.

We added playful touches like "likes to randomly dance down the aisles of Target" and "I'm a city girl with a country heart." I highlighted things I genuinely enjoyed—hiking, trying new restaurants, working out, reading in coffee shops, traveling, and spending time with friends and family. I consider myself a social person and wanted that to come through. My co-workers approved.

At the same time, I wanted to cut through the riffraff. I wasn't looking for another friend, a casual hook-up, or someone to randomly occupy my time. I'm more than capable of entertaining myself (almost too good at it), so I wanted someone who shared my values, enjoyed my company, and was genuinely interested in building something meaningful.

Then came the part where I had to list my "preferences"—age, height, ethnicity. For age, I was open to ten years older or five years younger, as long as it didn't feel like I was dating my dad or a young-tender².

I wasn't extremely particular on height. I figured if he was short, he could stand on his wallet (*I was joking . . . kinda*). Ethnicity was the one that gave me pause. I had preferences, sure, but I also didn't want to limit God's plan. For all I knew, He might have something different in mind. My only preferences were that he be gainfully employed, not juggling a gang of kids, and be attractive. (*I mean, let's be reasonable, right?*) So, I broadened my preferences to include everyone. Equal opportunity lover, right here.

Finally, the photos. I wanted to choose pictures showcasing my personality and my beauty. As a Black woman, my hairstyles are part of my culture and identity, and I wanted my profile to reflect that. I made sure to include variety: braids, long and straight, short and curly, and short and sleek. This way, no one would be surprised when they met me.

---

2   Young-tender = slang for a young'un, a younger person, a tender roni
    Tender Roni = Google Bobby Brown Tender Roni

With my profile up and running, I was ready to go. Friends had warned me not to get overwhelmed or discouraged by the underwhelming results. Honestly, I had no expectations. I saw online dating as just another avenue, a way of putting myself out there without limiting my options. If it worked, great. If not, well, my three months would buy me a few stories and a lesson learned.

The lessons started immediately.

Enter Arrogant Adam. Tall, Black and well... arrogant. At first glance, through his profile pictures, he was an immediate no. There was zero attraction, and I've always believed that without at least a little spark, it wasn't worth forcing conversation.

But my coworkers encouraged me to look at things differently. "You need practice," they said, "so go out with someone you're not that into—it'll take the pressure off." Fair point. Besides, I didn't want to judge a book solely by its cover. Sometimes personality can completely change the story.

He reached out first with a sweet compliment, and his initial messages were pleasant enough. So I decided he would be my trial date.

We kept it simple and agreed to meet for coffee one evening. I didn't bother dressing up, this wasn't that kind of date. I kept it cool and casual. As I walked up, I saw that he was indeed as tall as his profile stated. He bent over for an awkward side hug, and the scent of patchouli hit me like a wall.

Filters weren't as common then, but even so I hadn't noticed the texture of his skin in his pictures. Up close, it looked like someone had chewed on his cheeks before he shaved with the wrong razor, leaving intense bumps all the way down his neck—stopping only where his black choker necklace was. That, paired with a tight red Spiderman t-shirt and faded black jeans, completed the look.

When he asked if I wanted something to drink, I ordered a chai tea latte. He whipped out a large wad of cash and peeled off four dollars with unnecessary flair to pay for it. I turned my head and silently debated if it was too late to cancel my order and head home.

Sigh.

We sat outside since it was quieter than inside.

"You're really attractive," he said.

"Thank you," I responded with a smile.

"I normally don't date younger Black women, but when I saw you, I figured it would be worth a try."

I wasn't sure how to respond to that, so I just took a sip of my drink. If memory served, he was actually a few years younger than me.

"Yeah," he went on, "I was raised by my older sisters, all phenomenal Black women, and I would be willing to introduce someone like you to them. I think they are why I normally date older women. I just find that older women are more sophisticated and driven." He shrugged.

I took another sip.

"Bay Area women in general are just not normally at my caliber. They are too demanding and don't know their role."

I may or may not have choked on my tea at that point.

Arrogant Adam pressed on, rattling off everything he believed was wrong with women in the Bay and what he had experienced. I couldn't tell if he was trying to impress me or repulse me. The latter was winning by a landslide.

"I don't really do coffee either, but since you suggested it here, I figured it would be worth it."

"Mmm, really?" I thought, *If I leave now, I could be home in time to read a couple chapters of my new book.*

"I've seen you look at my necklace a couple of times." He picked up the emblem that was hanging off the front. It looked like the letters M and X mashed together. "This represents the fact that we are all one and thriving off one another's energy."

"I'm not sure I understand."

This was the invitation he needed. He launched into a lecture on creation, the world, and his theories on belief systems. I checked my watch.

"I really like how well you listen," he added.

"Mmm. Well, you know." *You haven't stopped talking and haven't asked me a single question about myself.*

"I think this is going to be something good."

"Do you?" I hoped my face didn't betray the horror I felt inside.

He nodded and sucked his teeth.

Dear God.

"Have you been on a lot of dates recently. Why are you so sure about me?" I asked.

"Think about it. I'm a tall Black man. I'm attractive and I have a job. I am desired. Women, y'all have it much harder. You have to wait to be chosen while men like me do the choosing. The hard part is over. I find you attractive."

"You have a point." He really did. Black men in the Bay Area are as sought after as a rent-controlled apartment with a dedicated parking space—EVERYONE wants one. This was probably one of the most intelligent things he said that night. Yet it was only half-true.

He saw his self-proclaimed attributes of being tall, dark, and handsome as prime dating currency. He knew the leverage he had, especially online. While I might have disagreed with how highly he rated himself, the man had confidence. His opinion was just valid. Mine was too—he was a waste of my time. He wasn't my cup of tea (pun intended), but that didn't mean maybe he was somebody else's.

For me, his "confidence" was a deterrent. I believed it was a mask for his insecurities. His tone was condescending and his views on women demeaning. He was one of those men who dated women but didn't truly like women for who they are and how they were created. The brother probably had some serious mommy issues.

My coffee cup felt lighter; time to wrap this up. I took one final sip of my drink, tilting my head back dramatically to get the last sip. "Well, I think I'll call it a night."

Should I go get McDonald's? I need some French fries to redeem this night.

"So soon?" Arrogant Adam raised an eyebrow. I think he was attempting to flirt. "Can I walk you to your car?"

"No! "The word came out a little fast. His eyes widened. "I'm right over here. I'll be fine." He stared at me long enough to make it uncomfortable.

"I have determined that I would like to see you again."

"Well, I don't think that would be a good idea." I stood to go. "Thank you for the tea. Wishing you all the best." I mumbled as I walked away without looking back. By the time I hightailed it to my car and collapsed in the front seat, exhaustion sank over me like a weighted blanket—only heavier because it came with discouragement.

Was this what online dating consisted of? How many of these experiences would I have to endure? I had heard so many stories about fun dates and cute guys. Yet from what I was seeing, between the "matches" showing up on my feed and the patchouli-scented disaster I'd just escaped—those stories felt like rare exceptions.

So I did what any woman in need of comfort would do: drove straight to McDonald's, grabbed an order of fries, and parked myself in my oversized chair at home. As I munched on the last salty remnants, I started unpacking my expectations.

I expected to go out on some dates with reasonably attractive men.

I expected to meet at least one person I was physically attracted to.

I expected to have an experience where I didn't want to run in the opposite direction, crawl under the covers, and wait for my future husband to knock on my door.

If it sounds like I spiraled into hopelessness, I did. This "there" everyone was referring to sucked. It sucked and I was disappointed. But disappointment has a way of forcing a deeper question: *what was my hope really in?* Was my hope in the random dating app, or in the One who is hope? When traveling through this dating wilderness, it can be easy to let expectations rest in the wrong place. My hope had to rest in God, not an algorithm.

I believe God wants us to wait well—no matter what we're waiting for. When we're waiting, whatever our "there" may be, we must learn contentment while we wait.

For some, waiting well may be online dating. That's between them and Jesus. For me, waiting well meant not scrambling to fix my singleness with quick solutions, or letting cultural pressure dictate my choices. It meant continuing to do the things that brought me joy, honoring God with my life, and remembering that the Holy Spirit—not a dating profile was my guide.

I did it. I put myself out there. But at the end of the day, my heart and my desires had to stay aligned with God. Because if my hope rested in Him, not in an app, then even a night like this one could be redeemed.

Lord,

I went to an event yesterday and, looking around, I saw married folks with their families and felt myself wanting that experience. I saw the moments of a sweet kiss or intimate touch. It all felt near and far at the same time.

There was a guy who caught my eye. He was an unconventionally cute . . . you know what I like (sidenote: there were A LOT of attractive men there. I rebuke the spirit of lust!) I had an acquaintance bring him over for an introduction and turns out, he was one of those deep thinkers and wanted to have a real conversation to see what I was about mentally and intellectually. I met him where he was at and he was pleasantly pleased. However, when it came to spiritual compatibility, we fell short and my pleasure dissipated. He was taught religion growing up and was never taught about relationship. Therefore, he didn't believe in Jesus Christ and felt like the Bible was fiction.

Sigh. Same ol' story, Lord. Same ol' story.

We even talked about dating with the abstinence of sex. (Yep, we covered a lot of topics.) He wanted to go there, so I went there. He was trying to argue the case around why abstinence is not natural. I don't know why I waste my time in these conversations. I wasn't about to convince this stranger that I consider myself worth waiting for.

Lord, this is all the more reason why I would have to be with someone who loves Jesus. While he may struggle with the abstinence part (like we all do), he would at least understand its origins and the premise of it. I believe he will respect it too.

The enemy subtly whispered to me, "Would it hurt just to sleep with him once? You need someone to redeem you from Entertaining Eddie."

And Lord, for a second, I considered it.

Forgive me.

That consideration was just as fleeting as the experience would have been. I'm not looking for fleeting. I'm looking for sustenance, longevity, covenant.

Father, thank you for blessing me to remain firm in my faith and not to be shaken by the desires of my flesh. Thank you for allowing me to be planted on the rock of salvation and grace. I am more than my body and I am obedient to the Lord.

Father, I vowed not to obsess over waiting for my hubby, and you have allowed me to live such an abundant life as I wait on the manifestation of your promise. So, Lord, I pray that my future hubby will be willing and able to date me with abstinence from sex and be happy about it. Help us to put boundaries in place that serve and honor you. I pray we feel comfortable around each other and can build true intimacy together. And Father, I pray that once our union is formed, our physical intimacy exceeds both of our expectations.

Amen

Chapter 9

Over Before it Even Starts

Carrie
Girl! I met a cute guy.

My Sister
Oooh, tell me more.

He was cool. Somewhat older. I was at a spot I had never been to and a crowd I don't normally associate with.

um, where were you at?

Let's not worry about the details. He's tall, kinda quiet but sweet. Has two kids.

...

I know. You know I'm praying about him first.

> ok, well- see how things go.

Less than 24 hours later.

Carrie
> Girl, never mind. 😐

My Sister
> Oop. Okay. God answered that prayer fast.

My Lord,

I know you're sovereign and all my days were planned out before I was born. But I'm struggling in this dating area. Well, more specifically . . . I'm struggling to trust You with my dating life.

I, I . . . I just feel like I haven't seen You show up for me in this particular area. When it comes to work or career, friendships, and financial provision, You show up repeatedly and its always so clear. When I wanted that one role, You made it clear that it wasn't for me and then You opened up a new door that was perfect for me.

But in dating . . . sigh. This season is lasting much longer than I thought. I'm trying to trust You. But I can't help but wonder—where is my exceedingly abundantly?

Is my perspective just off?

Chapter 10

Unexpected Answers to Prayers – Part 1

"Hey girl, I've been getting all kind of comments on the pictures I posted from last night." My childhood bestie usually stuck to texting, so when my phone rang, I was caught off guard. The excitement in her voice told me there was more to the story.

She was talking about the belated fortieth birthday surprise we had pulled off for her—a night out with a group of girlfriends. Like most of the world, COVID had hijacked her original plans, so we decided to make up for it. The theme was animal print and cocktail dresses. Let's just say, I understood the assignment.

I put on my high-waisted support underwear (don't knock it until you've tried it), drank coffee after 12 p.m. so I could stay up past 10 p.m. and made my way to dinner. The venue was one of those hot, new Instagram-worthy restaurants with wicker swings, banana bikes with cute baskets, and neon signs plastered against fake grass walls. Everything dripped in fuchsia décor.

I was with a group of mothers and aunties whose eyes widened as each new crowd walked by. The young women wore tight, short dresses that left little to the imagination, reminding us of when we'd worn the same. Their dates wore shiny shirts unbuttoned halfway down and circular sunglasses with red lenses.

Every thirty minutes, the DJ cranked up the volume and blasted the top birthday songs. Servers paraded trays of cupcakes and shots balanced with sparklers, delivering them to tables of shrieking, woot-woot-ing women while friends captured every moment for Instagram stories guaranteed to cause FOMO.

The food was wildly overpriced and painfully mediocre. By the third birthday song, the music was deafening, my support wear was staging a revolt, and the caffeine was fading fast.

We were officially old.

But old or not, we laughed loudly and yelled at one another in a herculean effort to make conversation over the pulsing bass in the music. My childhood BFF, Eva, and I caught up on the highlights of one another's lives while some of the others shared updates on career moves, kids' sporting events, and the occasional "you'll never guess who I ran into." With ringing ears and full bellies, we had our own social media moments and captured plenty of pictures. The great thing about celebrating a fortieth birthday is by the time you turn forty, you know your angles. The pictures turned out cute, and we felt good about calling it a night.

Eva wasted no time posting several of the pictures on her social media pages. Her call the next day was to tell me about one persistent guy who left several comments about me in her DMs.

"I don't know if you remember this one guy as he didn't go to high school with us, but we knew of him. He was in your brother fraternity and went to the university up north. He lives in Nap now. His name is Messy Marvin."

"Doesn't ring a bell but then again, you know I never remember people. Feels a little too close for comfort."

"I know, I know. I'll send you a screenshot of his profile picture. There is just one thing."

"Okay . . ." I waited, unsure as to what Eva was going to share. I figured maybe he dated someone we knew, especially since he still lived in our hometown, where it seemed as if people were recycled through the single-to-relationship-back-to-single factory.

"He's short and he has a son."

"That's two things. And how short?"

"Well, you liked Entertaining Eddie and he's short."

"True. I don't mind a short man. He can stand on his wallet. But how short is he?"

Eva bypassed my shallow comment, half agreeing, and said, "I'm not sure. He's standing next to his son in the picture I just sent over which makes him look even shorter."

I pulled up the picture. Messy Marvin was short. Short and stocky. From my quick scroll through his other photos, I'd guess maybe five-foot-eight on a good day. I wasn't impressed by the pictures, but I tried not to make my only impression based on pictures.

Eva, on the other hand, had done her homework. She rattled off information she'd uncovered from her own social media stalking:

- He owned a house in the nicer, higher-class part of town.

- He had sole custody of his son, who was a sophomore in high school.
- He identified as a Christian.
- He was funny and liked to crack jokes.
- He played high school and college football.
- He worked in finance and had a master's degree in finance.
- He never posted pictures with women.
- He looked like he had a solid relationship with his mom.
- Most importantly, he thought I was gorgeous and was eager to get to know me.

Note: Every girl needs a friend whose an amateur sleuth when it comes to potential men to date. Eva knew everything but his social security number and if I had pressed her, she might have found that out too.

"Mmm, so what have you told him about me?"

"I just gave him your social media handle. I think that will tell him everything he needs to know."

Smart move. My social media was a curated glimpse into my life, but most of all, it was an alternative way of marketing my blog. And my blog was where I laid out a lot about my faith walk and dating as a Christian woman. If Messy Marvin truly wanted to know me, all it took was a click.

"Cool. If he's interested, he'll reach out." I sent a quick prayer to God about His will being done and left it at that.

Years of singleness had taught me not to get my hopes up when a friend called and said, "I know someone who thinks you're cute" or "There is someone I want you to meet." Half the time, the guy never reached out, or the friend conveniently forgot to mention he was twenty-five years my senior, or he had five children by four different women. Even worse, some thought they were doing me a favor by introducing someone who didn't share the most important thing to me: a genuine walk with Christ.

One sorority sister and her husband tried hard to introduce me to compatible guys. One was a football player—quiet, nice, but slightly boring. Another was a novice entrepreneur (also short, go figure), but he just wasn't interested and our communication fizzled before a date ever happened. I'm concluding we ghosted one another (*if that is even possible*).

Of course, I'd seen matchmaking success stories and even played matchmaker myself once and watched a friend marry the man I introduced her to. But I wasn't excited about Messy Marvin. I forgot about him until I received a direct message on social media a few weeks later.

Messy Marvin: Hello, Ms. Carrie. You may not know me, but I had inquired about you through Eva. I am reaching out in hopes of getting to know you and growing a friendship. I hope all is well and I hear from you soon."

I was surprised to see that this message showed up under a previous message exchange with this same person from seven years prior. The older thread of messages read:

> **M:** How's it going? I work with your cousin and saw a picture of you on her desk. I told her I just had to meet you.

Me: That must have been some picture 😊

M: Oh, it was. Are you making it back home to Nap anytime soon?

Seven years ago, I had read it but never responded. Yet, here he was, trying again. (*Well, at least the man knew what he liked and was consistent.*)

I didn't immediately respond. Instead, I went full detective—scrolling through his recent posts. He was active online, posting jokes and funny stories throughout the day. I noticed plenty of mutual friends and realized we probably crossed paths at some point in college. I decided to respond and flex my flirting muscles.

C: Hi there. I heard you've been asking about me. Was wondering if you were going to summon the courage to reach out . . .

Messy Marvin quickly hearted the message and responded.

MM: so basically, you've been talking about me already? That's good to hear.

C: LOL. You've been discussed.

MM: Good things, I hope?

C: That's still up for debate.

Our flirting continued back and forth for the rest of the evening. The next day he asked if he could give me a call. I agreed—partly curious and partly hopeful. After all, he'd made me laugh through text, and laughter is never a bad start.

Messy Marvin did not disappoint. He was lively, funny, and easy to talk to.

"So, you know you've reached out to me before, right?" I asked.

"What do you mean? We met in college or something?"

"Nope, you hit me up on Facebook telling me you saw a picture of me on Tia's desk."

Silence. I checked my phone to see if I lost the call.

"Yooooo, you're Tia's cousin?"

"Yep."

"Does she know you're talking to me?"

"Should she? Did y'all date or something?"

"Not at all. She didn't want you to talk to me and said you were too good for me. Which, at the time, you probably were. But that's craaazy."

"I know, right?"

"Wait, what did we talk about?"

"Eh, not much. It was short and sweet." I quickly relayed our exchange to him and he responded with, "You left me 'on read' then ghosted me?"

"Was ghosting really a thing back then?"

"Don't change the subject, young lady! We could be married with little juniors running around by now. But nooo, you were too bougie for me."

I feigned horror, and we had a good laugh.

"Well, I like what I like," he said.

"I guess you do."

I had to admit, I kind of liked the fact that we had come full circle. It was nice to feel desired and sought after so blatantly, but I wasn't going to let that flattery cloud my discernment.

"I think there is something you need to know, though." It was my turn to come clean. In my stalking, I realized that our paths had crossed more than I cared to admit. He had gone to the same school as Smitty Stevie, and they were in the same fraternity but a few years apart (*I had a type too.*) Smitty Stevie participated in initiating Messy Marvin and his brothers, which meant that when I was hanging around Smitty Stevie, I'd probably run into Messy Marvin too.

This felt a bit icky even if it was over a decade ago. So, I decided to rip the Band-Aid off and said, "I used to date-slash-kick it and sleep with Smitty Stevie."

"He's weird. You liked him?"

"I did. But I wanted to make sure you knew. Living in Nap, I'm sure this wouldn't be the first time this has come up for you." I threw in some shade about our hometown, hoping to deflect from the awkwardness of it all.

"I guess you're right." I was surprised at how easily he conceded without much sarcasm that I was already used to from him.

"Wait!" I blurted out. "Have *you* slept with any of my sorority sisters?" I had eighteen other sorority sisters who crossed with me and even though we didn't talk every day, I was never going to entertain anyone they had even kissed—no matter how long ago it was.

He chuckled before answering, "Got ya nervous, huh?"

"A lil' bit."

"Nah, girl. Your line was too fine for me. As an athlete, I only messed with other athletes in school."

"What about after?" I was covering all my bases. I wasn't sure if he lived by the "omission isn't lying" rule, so I was sure to be thorough.

"Nope. I didn't date anyone from your school at all. I kept it closer to home than you did." I heard the smirk in his voice and allowed his dig. He was in good spirits and quickly steered the conversation forward.

He shared more about his son and how he hadn't even known he had a son until the kid was two years old. A fling from college had followed him into young adulthood, forcing him to grow up faster than he had planned. Things accelerated again when he took full custody of his son once he started high school. Ever risk-adverse to baby-momma-drama, I took the opportunity to ask about his relationship with the mother.

"She's married with other kids and supports when she feels like it."

"What does support look like exactly?"

"I try to be mindful of how to speak about her, especially in front of him, but I wish she did more considering his age and how impressionable he is."

As Messy Marvin continued, I found myself admiring the maturity in how he handled things. From what he described, there was no lingering attraction or wishful thinking, just two people living separate lives, engaging only when necessary. I knew I was hearing only one side of the story, but still, it struck me as steady and responsible.

As with every man I met, I prayed about Messy Marvin. I asked the Holy Spirit if I should lower any of my walls to let him in. I didn't hear a clear answer, but I knew dating required risk, so I proceeded with caution.

Within our first few weeks of knowing each other, I shared my concerns about long distance and made it clear I had no plans to move back to Indiana. He acknowledged my hesitation and shared his plans to relocate to California after his son graduated high school. He was a huge football fan and an even bigger fan of one of the Southern California universities.

Since I traveled frequently for work, we discussed leveraging our personal and work travel to spend in-person time together. He assured me that if we chose to do this long-distance relationship, our time together would be more intentional and meaningful.

Knowing he had a plan to be in California long-term, our daily communication settled into a rhythm. We Facetimed between meetings when we could, but mostly texted. The three-hour time difference was a beast. He was an early riser; I was a night owl. By the time I was ready to have a real conversation, he was usually winding down for bed. More than once, he went dark and stopped responding to my texts around 7 p.m. PST. I would then wake up to a text sent at 1 or 2 a.m. my time with him apologizing, saying he had fallen asleep but was up for his morning workout.

Messy Marvin was full of personality and constantly cracked jokes. Sometimes, I couldn't tell his jokes from the truth. His wit was entertaining, but I stayed guarded. I needed to learn more about his character and integrity. Too often, his words and actions didn't align. I kept my walls up and quietly stored those observations in the back of my mind.

A few things stood out.

"I don't drink," he would say. Then he would call me after a night, his voice clearly slurred, or post on social media about what he was drinking that night.

"I love church," he'd claim—yet week after week, he never attended or streamed church service at home. I don't believe church attendance makes someone a Christian, but being part of a faith community is vital for growth, accountability, and encouragement. Church has always been central to my life, and I knew I wanted a partner who shared that commitment.

"I'm social, but I don't have many friends." He admitted. And that much was true. He didn't maintain strong relationships with men in his life. His bond with his brothers was strained, and not long after we met, he had a falling out with his best friend. I didn't expect him to be popular, but I couldn't help questioning where the structure for growth was without close friendships, mentors, and accountability.

Messy Marvin did have redeeming qualities that kept me from immediately walking away. Beyond his humor and charm, he had a big heart for kids and was a loving family man. He volunteered as a coach for a school football team and poured extra time into the younger boys in his family, determined to show them they could grow up differently than he had. His own upbringing was difficult, and I admired the way he used that pain as motivation to give back. He was also very handy around the house and maintained a gorgeous home. He was always showing me a new project he was working on. On top of that, he was focused on his health. He cooked and liked to send me pictures of his latest meal creations.

I used to tease, asking how he hadn't found a wife yet, considering all that he offered. In our hometown, it was rare to meet someone his age that had never been married.

After nearly two months of talking, my work travels were taking me to the Midwest. It seemed like the perfect opportunity to finally meet in person. I planned an extended weekend with my sister, who lived just two-and-a-half hours away from him.

We had planned out the whole weekend. He would come down on a Saturday morning and stay until Monday. He booked a hotel while I would stay with my sister and her family. I had explained my commitment to be abstinent, and he assured me he was in full support.

A week before the trip, he asked me if I would be willing to stay with him at least one night. I figured one night wouldn't hurt, and I felt that since we had been clear about our boundaries, it was a risk I was willing to take. Expecting him to drive me back to my sister's house after hours of being together didn't feel realistic. We had been getting along well—I hoped that chemistry would translate in person.

The night before we were going to see one another, he was winning me over with his excitement and kind words about looking forward to our time together.

"One more sleep!!!" he texted.

His enthusiasm stirred up my own—mixed with equal parts curiosity and skepticism. I wasn't sure if I'd be physically attracted to him. What if he couldn't kiss or had bad breath? What if he was socially awkward in person or rude to others?

My mind spun through the what-ifs, and I had to stop myself before I talked myself out of the whole weekend. If I was going to date, I had to actually interact with people—not just imagine worst-case scenarios

That night, I went to bed with cautious anticipation about what the weekend could hold.

The next morning, I woke up to a text.

> **MM:** It's so nice to text you and know we're on the same time zone.
>
> **Me:** I agree! Good morning.
>
> **MM:** For now, I had a bit of a hiccup.
>
> **MM:** My nephew tested positive for COVID.

My stomach dropped.

> **Me:** Wasn't he just over your house two days ago?
>
> **MM:** Yep. He was here last night too. I'm going to get tested now.
>
> **Me:** Hmm. Okay.
>
> **MM:** Whatchu thinking?
>
> **Me:** I can't afford to get my sister's family sick.
>
> **MM:** I know. That's why I'm getting tested. I'll let you know as soon as I get the results.

My heart sank. It would be so disappointing to come all this way and not get to see him. Still, I wasn't willing to risk my health or the health of my sister and her family.

So I decided to be productive while I waited. I opened my Bible, determined to edify my Spirit just in case some fleshly temptation crept in. Messy Marvin wasn't ultimately my concern—I was. It had been a long time since I had been physically close with a guy. While I hadn't had sex, I had stretched the limits more than I cared to admit. In past situations, my body did the talking, and I didn't want that to happen again. I was still figuring out how to date and be completely abstinent, which meant instead of asking God how much I could do, I was trying to err on the side of caution and not do anything. Based on what I'd seen about Messy Marvin, he would respect me, but he wasn't going to be the one holding back. That was going to be up to me and the Holy Spirit.

Two hours passed, and I hadn't heard back from him. By then, he should have been on the road for thirty minutes. I sent him a text.

Me: Um, you good?

No response.
I called him.
No answer.

My family was getting started with their day and began asking me what my plans were. I didn't have an answer, which was beginning to irritate me. I encouraged them not to worry about me and go about their day.

Another hour passed before I received a response.

MM: Sorry. My test was negative but I'm having some trouble getting in touch with my son's mom. She is supposed to pick him up after he gets off work but she is not confirming.

Me: Oh no! Did y'all make these arrangements ahead of time?

MM: Of course. But you know she is flaky at times.

Me: Got it.

MM: I'm leaving here in 30-45 minutes regardless though. I'll hit you when I jump on the road.

Ninety minutes went by without a word from Messy Marvin. At this point, I was furious. I called again with no response.

If we couldn't make time this weekend, dating long distance wasn't worth the hassle. I had no interest in pursuing a relationship where we never got the chance to see one another. Also, his lack of communication was appalling. I felt my walls inching up higher.

Finally, his name popped up on my phone screen.

"I'm an hour away." I could tell he was in the car, but based on how the day was going so far, I knew he wasn't an hour away.

"You're lying" was all I could say. My insides were starting to shake, which meant my anger was flaring, and I had to clip my words to ensure I didn't overreact or say the wrong thing.

"Why would I lie? For real. I'm passing . . ." He named an exit that was closer than an hour from my sister's house.

"You didn't think to call, text, or anything?"

"I didn't want you to tell me not to come. I can tell you're pissed. But I'm making it work."

"What does that mean exactly?" I was feeling a bit bamboozled. Things weren't adding up, and I couldn't tell if he was simply bad at time management or if something else was going on. Red flags seemed to be waiving left and right, and part of me wanted to cut my losses right then and there.

To calm down, I called one of my girlfriends and explained the whole debacle. I talked fast and paced around my sister's house. I told her how I was ready to throw the whole weekend away and chalk up the last couple of months to proof as to why I don't want a long-distance relationship. She listened and then gently reminded me that when a man has kids, he can't get up and go whenever he wanted. She encouraged me to give him grace, hear him out, and remember he was driving two hours to see me. When he got here, my attitude would determine how the rest of the weekend played out.

I heard her but I still wanted to pout. I couldn't pout long because shortly after ending my call, I received a text from him saying, "I'm here."

I did my best to fix my face. My friend was right. Now that he was here, I didn't want the whole weekend to go to waste. My reception of him would be the determining factor.

Walking out to the driveway, I let a smile spread over my face. He was standing outside his car and when he saw my smile, his shoulders dropped. I watched the tension drain from his body as he let out a breath and smiled back. When we embraced, he picked me up and spun me around.

Soon after, we were on the road and headed to the hotel. Messy Marvin shared more details about why he was late. He provided an elaborate story about his nephew, getting his son tested, and ensuring his son could still go to work and that his mother knew to pick him up after work. His son didn't have his driver's license yet, and Messy Marvin wasn't comfortable leaving him alone all night.

"I don't want to get the call that the house is burning down while I'm trying to romanticize you."

"Aw yeah, that's what you'll be trying to do?"

"Nah, just trying to get out of the doghouse and ensure you like me as much as I like you."

"What makes you think you're in the doghouse? Have I not been pleasant since the moment we laid eyes on each other?"

"True, you have. But I could tell your anger was simmering."

"You cannot. You just know you could have handled that better. Communication goes a long way with me."

"You're right. Lesson learned. I apologize. I'll not make assumptions next time and just tell you everything up front."

We joked and laughed the whole drive there, as conversation flowed easily. After we were checked into the hotel, we kept a chill vibe. However, if I had a chance to redo the evening, I probably wouldn't have agreed to share a hotel room. It turned out to be far harder than I imagined to draw lines once we were next to each other in the same bed.

I had gone in with pure intentions, convinced temptation wouldn't be an issue. What I didn't account for was how quickly hunger grows when the opportunity to satisfy it is right in front of you. What ultimately stopped me from going further boiled down to two things.

First was the emptiness from the fooling around we did. There was no fullness, no sweetness, no closeness. The warmth

I had once associated with intimacy was nowhere to be found. Instead, every touch felt hollow—transactional. He didn't know me, and I didn't know him. Even the kiss, something that should've sparked connection, carried no emotion.

Second, I had asked several people to hold me accountable. I didn't want to give a recap of the evening and admit that I messed up. I wouldn't lie and it would be written all over my face anyway.

The "second-and-a-half" reason was I had big doubts that it would be worth it. Sometimes you just know. And this was one of those times. I wasn't about to trade my peace—or my conviction—for what I suspected would end in disappointment. I was not willing to sign up for a tragic experience in the end.

Waste of time and spiritual compromise? No thanks.

Before we fell asleep, he received a text from his son. I noticed him trying to mask his reaction, but I wasn't sure what it was.

The next morning, he explained that he needed to get home earlier than planned. His son ended up spending the night alone, and now he needed a ride to some type of activity.

I understood that his responsibilities as a father came first, but I couldn't help feeling perturbed that our "two-and-a-half days" had been reduced to less than twenty-four hours. I knew better than to share my selfish thoughts and remembered my friend's advice—when children are in the mix, priorities shift.

So we tried to make the best of what time remained. We squeezed in a workout together and brunch. I could tell he was trying to overcompensate for the short weekend because he was being extra complimentary, which fell flat. He was also cracking more jokes in an effort to lighten the mood. He would often ask what I was thinking about or share random stories about the last time he visited that city to keep the conversation steady.

When he dropped me off at my sister's house, I gave him what I figured was going to be our last hug. His actions and explanations didn't align clearly, and I wasn't in the mood to probe. If he wasn't truly available for a long-distance relationship, I wasn't going to add myself as another responsibility on his already messy plate.

Later that night, I received a text that read, "What did I do wrong?"

Messy Marvin's perceptiveness and willingness to address conflict was a plus. I just wasn't sure how to respond. We weren't deep enough in for "expectations," yet I couldn't shake my doubt about his honesty. Either way, the weekend had left me disappointed. My defenses shot back up, and the wall around my heart was fully erected.

Chapter 11

Unexpected Answers to Prayers – Part 2

My eagerness to walk away was thwarted after sharing a weekend recap with others. The consensus? Messy Marvin had responded the way a responsible father should. And if there was any dishonesty in the mix, it would come out in time. The bigger question was whether I was truly willing to date a man with kids, because kids will always be the priority.

In other words, I couldn't be a brat if I was going to date a man with kids.

Fair enough.

So, Messy Marvin and I resumed our dance of texts and random FaceTime calls. His compliments grew bolder, and his declarations of liking me stronger. I even talked with his son from time to time. He sent me sweet R&B songs, initiated deeper conversations, and became more consistent in his communication.

On the surface, he was showing up differently. But I still felt like things lacked depth. He shared stories—about his family, his thoughts—but they were often repetitive. Rarely did he ask questions that dug into what mattered to me. The gap between us stretched wider with each shallow exchange.

I made conscious efforts to close it, to reciprocate by sharing more of myself. But it often felt forced, like I was spoon-feeding him information instead of conversation flowing naturally. He claimed he preferred to "observe" rather than ask direct questions, but how much can you observe through text threads and brief calls? His bold declarations that I was "right" for him felt empty when I knew he didn't actually know me.

We had already planned to see each other in the fall for his annual California football game trip, but two months felt too far away. Thankfully, my work was taking me to the East Coast—Philadelphia and New York—within a ten-day time span. I figured we could spend some time together and see what this could really be. I suggested that he come to Philadelphia for the weekend.

"No pressure but if you could make it work, that would be cool." In truth, I expected him to make it work.

"I'll try to make that work," he said. "I just found out I have to go to Florida for work the week before, but it shouldn't be a problem."

"Well, let me know. My work trip is booked. No matter what, I will be in Philly for the weekend. It's my first time being there, so I want to have some fun exploring the city."

"I'd like to explore the city too. I like that you like to travel."

I sent him my flight information and left it at that. Honestly, things didn't look too promising. With his work trip to Florida just days before, and knowing how hard it was for him to arrange support for his son, I wasn't sure he could actually make it happen.

Thankfully, his mom was staying at his house while he traveled, so at least his son's schedule would be minimally impacted.

To my surprise, the following week, he confirmed that he booked a flight to meet me in Philly for the weekend. He said his flight was scheduled to arrive about an hour before mine, so he'd wait for me at the airport.

The weekend felt like a defining weekend for us. I was looking forward to more in-depth talks and a chance to be around one another and really connect.

From time to time, he'd send messages like, "Let me in, Carrie," or ask, "Are you mine? Because I'm yours." I didn't always have a response. I was trying to let him in. Inviting him to spend the weekend with me was my earnest attempt. After this weekend, I'd be all in or all out.

In the days leading up to the trip, he sent thoughtful messages about being excited to see me. He also sent me pictures from his own travels and would call and say how he missed my smile and just wanted to hear my voice.

And so, as I sat on the plane preparing for takeoff, I repeated the prayer that had been on my lips all week:

> *Lord, thank you for the opportunity to travel. I pray your traveling mercies cover us as we fly. Please allow me to see what I need to see and hear what I need to hear. If this relationship is not your plan for me, let me know and make it plain. I submit this weekend to you.*

Almost six hours later, I landed. Immediately, something felt off. A stirring in the pit of my stomach whispered, *"He's probably not even here."* I took my phone out of airplane mode. Messages and emails rolled in—but nothing from Messy Marvin.

The stirring grew stronger and my heartbeat quickened. My brow furrowed as I sent the obligatory messages about my safe arrival to family and friends. Then typed my message to him.

"Hey! Are you here?"

I waited.

No response.

My flight arrived later than planned, so maybe he was waiting at the gate. Maybe his flight was delayed. Or cancelled. There had to be a logical explanation. Let me not jump to conclusions.

I deplaned and scanned the crowd as I headed to baggage claim. He was nowhere in sight. My anger began to simmer.

I repeatedly checked my phone to ensure I hadn't missed something.

No voicemails and no other text messages had come through.

I felt a headache coming on. The simmer was turning into a boil.

Finally, as I stood at the carousel waiting for my bag, I received a series of short text messages that read:

> **MM:** Don't hate me.
>
> **MM:** I missed my flight. I must have left my ID at CVS when I went to get a COVID test to ensure I was safe to come out there.
>
> **MM:** I got all the way to the airport and realized I didn't have my ID.
>
> **MM:** But don't worry, I was able to get flight credit. I will go to the DMV first thing in the morning.

MM: They are not open 24 hours. They open at 7 am.

MM: I'll be there at 8. I should make my flight.

MM: This is not reflective of my character. Don't hate me!!

My insides began to shake. My anger was boiling over. I retrieved my luggage and called his phone.

No response.

The fact that he hadn't picked up the phone to at least explain the situation was baffling. While I waited for my taxi, I tried calling again.

No response.

My mind went back to how he handled our first weekend together. Was he ignoring my messages because he knew I was upset, figuring I'd tell him not to come? I reasoned with myself that maybe him arriving a day later would be to my benefit. I had an early start for work and didn't need distractions. A good night's sleep would help me reset. So, I silenced my notifications and laid my head down, choosing not to think too much about it.

The following morning, I awoke to a vague message about how he hoped that I wouldn't judge him based on "this one mishap." I wasn't even sure which mishap he was referring to because there was more than one. Between his silence, lack of clarity, and the complete absence of follow-through, I received the answer I was waiting on.

He wasn't coming.

No calls. No texts. No explanations. He just . . . didn't show up.

Messy Marvin had stood me up in the city of brotherly love. *(Thought it felt anything but to me.)*

I wish I could say I shook it off and kept moving. But instead, I sat on the hotel bed, called my sister, and cried. I felt humiliated. Hurt. Shocked. I had never been stood up before, let alone in another city. Yes, I was there for work, but I hadn't planned to spend the weekend by myself. Yet, there I was. Alone. Humiliated. Frustrated.

I was humiliated that I had believed the lies of some man that wasn't worthy of my company nor my time, and frustrated that I hadn't seen it coming. His disregard for my feelings and my time hit me like a punch I wasn't ready for. I retraced the week in my mind, scanning for clues or red flags I had missed. I scrolled through our text conversation searching for answers.

Did I see the signs and dismiss them, calling it "staying open" or "not being judgmental"? Maybe. The truth was, I had been fighting against the lie that I was too difficult to love, that I required too much. So I tried to be chill, patient, open—even when deep down, I knew he wasn't meeting the standard. And now I berated myself for not jumping ship sooner.

I replayed every moment I'd felt the nudge to call it quits but didn't. Every time his words and actions didn't line up. Every time he said he would call but sent a text instead. I thought about how his compliments leaned more on my looks than on my character or my mind. I recalled how he couldn't maintain any relationships with siblings or friends in his life. The nudges had been there all along, but I ignored them.

Looking back, I know now those nudges weren't just gut feelings. They were the Holy Spirit telling me that I don't have to settle. It was ok to have standards. That wasn't judging, it was using wisdom.

And before the enemy could twist this into self-condemnation, trying to make me feel foolish for trusting God with my dating life—I realized something.

This weekend was an answered prayer.

I had asked the Holy Spirit to close the door if Messy Marvin wasn't the one. And He did. Not in the way I imagined, but in a way I couldn't ignore. Being stood up hurt, but it had to happen. It was God's mercy, sparing me from more wasted time, drama, and regret.

Messy Marvin was not for me. God had made it crystal clear.

As I stood in that hotel room, staring out at the bustling city and the bright sunshine, I had a choice to make. I could wallow in humiliation, and let the enemy beat me up with *should've, would've, could've*— or I could see this for what it really was, a blessing in disguise. I was safe. I was healthy. I was in a new city with a corporate per diem (*c'mon, somebody*).

Things could've been much worse.

I laced up my walking shoes, stepped out into the sunshine, put on a smile, and chose to feast on good food and new sights instead of disappointment.

Later that afternoon, as I recounted everything to my mentor, she confirmed that God had answered my prayer. "It's not lost on me that you experienced this in the city of brotherly love. Go do what you would normally do and let the Lord love on you in His own way," she said.

So that's exactly what I did. I wandered up cobblestone alleyways, ducked in and out of shops, and paused to take in the sound of live performances in the park. With every step, a peace began to stir so sweetly within me.

I lifted my face to the sky, smiling at how much God had spared me from—future heartbreak, more inconsistency, and the kind of confusion I had already lived through too many times. I didn't know exactly what that weekend *could* have held if Messy Marvin had shown up, but I did know what it didn't hold: God's best for me.

Instead, I felt His love in the simplest ways—every time I exchanged a smile with a stranger, discovered a new historic landmark, or sat still with the sunshine warming my face. The very city that could have been marked by rejection was now filled with reminders of His affection.

Around 45 Days Later (after 11 p.m. PST)

Messy Marvin: This ain't the liquor talking . . . I OWE you an apology.

Me: sounds like the liquor talking.

MM: This was the weekend. I was going to come out to your house.

We were supposed to go to the football game together.

MM: I can explain. Lemme explain.

Me: Listen, you don't have to do this. It just wasn't meant to be.

MM: 😭😭😭

MM: send me your email. It will make much more sense.

I sent him my email in hopes of pacifying his late-night, emoji-filled drunk texts.

I checked my email to see that he had forwarded an email exchange between him and his manager. I cringed in second-hand embarrassment. His email read like someone who had never been in a professional setting. The grammar was careless, the tone defensive, and the message was essentially one long argument against his own manager's corrective feedback. He shifted blame, insisting the issue wasn't his responsibility and that his leader was the one at fault.

The tone of language seemed oddly similar to the flurry of incoherent phrases he was texting me.

Me: I'm not sure what the point of that email was but let me stop you now. You're messy and this is not a good look.

He responded with more confusing phrases and comments, followed by a host of emojis.

Me: You should probably sleep off whatever it is you're on. You'll regret this in the morning.

MM: This was the weekend. I was going to come out to your house.

I never received a call the following day, but I also didn't expect one. I have no doubt that he read his text exchange with sober eyes and decided it would be best to leave things as they were.

Nine Months Later

Messy Marvin: Hello, is there any chance of repair or friendship?

Me: Nah. I believe what people show me about themselves. You never even offered an apology for the shenanigans you pulled. Be blessed. ✌️

I took a screenshot of the conversation and forwarded it to my sister with the note:

Me: I wanted to respond with some other choice words. Sigh. Being holy is a thing.

Sister: That's the Holy Spirit doing what it's supposed to do.

Me: true dat

Dear Lord,

I love you. You are my Protector, my Sun, and my Shield.

I'm sorry I ever doubted you. Please forgive me for saying that you have not shown up in my dating life. How silly of me. You've been showing up this entire time.

I realize that I based my trust of you on how I wanted you to show up and completely discounted the fact that you have been protecting me and shielding me from myself and others.

You answer prayers in a way that we need, not just want. I'm so grateful you are a sovereign God. You see all and know all.

Thank you for your protection and not allowing me to settle for less than your best. Thank you for your mercy and grace. I forgive Messy Marvin, and I trust you to keep me, love me, and care for me in ways that only you can.

Amen.

Chapter 12

Where do I Draw the Panty Line?

I was sitting at my cubicle when my coworker, Linda, ran over and said, "Did you see that guy who was walking around the floor with Pete?"

Another team member chimed in, "I almost fainted when I saw him!"

Our department was primarily women, and the only men present either identified as part of the LGBTQ+ community or were married. Translation: if an attractive, seemingly single, straight guy sets foot on our floor, it became breaking news. I quickly found out that he was Black or Black-adjacent, and with me being the only single Black woman on the team, everyone made sure I knew about him.

I pretended to need something from my boss so I could scope a view of the floor, but I didn't see anyone as I walked to her desk. No mystery man in sight. I shrugged and returned to my chair, ignoring the way my coworkers' heads swiveled toward me, expectant like they were waiting for the big reveal.

Pete was one of my direct reports and his seat was on the opposite side of my cubicle. He sat down and swiveled his seat toward me with a smirk.

"Did you see my friend who came by the office to see me?"

"No, I didn't."

"Oh. Well, we ran into each other in the city not too long ago. We used to work together, and he asked me where I was working now. Once I told him, he said he wanted to come by and see the office. He's apparently been trying to get a job here for a while now. I showed him around the floor and took him to the cafe."

"That's nice of you. What department is he interested in?"

"Loss prevention. He would be great for it too. He used to be a police officer."

"That's cool." I kept working but felt Pete staring at me.

"Are you sure you didn't see him?" he asked.

I side-eyed him, but before I could answer, Linda slid up to his desk. "Spill it. How do you know the hot guy, and is he gay or straight?"

Pete looked at me with a slick smile on his face and answered, "Straight. I was just asking Carrie if she saw him."

"No, she didn't but she should have. That man is gorgeous!"

I shook my head. "Y'all are silly." This time I really did need to talk to my boss, so I headed towards her office. As I stood in the doorway, mid-thought, I glanced to my right—and lost my train of thought. Striding towards me was this six-foot-four, muscular, bald-headed, clean-shaven, broad-chested man who was dipped in caramel with a killer smile framed by dimples.

Pete got up and met him in the hallway.

"My God, who is that?" my boss, a woman who had been with her live-in boyfriend for several years, asked.

"Um, I think that's Pete's friend who is trying to get a job here."

Normally my awkwardness went through the roof when I saw a hot guy, but not this time. I looked him directly in his eyes and smiled. He smiled back. The moment lingered just long enough for me to know he kept watching as I turned back to my boss, pretending to finish our conversation—really just telling her to *stop staring before we got caught*. By the time he left the floor, a collective squeal rose from the women in my department.

When I walked back to my desk, they were all waiting with the we-know-you-saw-him-this-time look. I ignored their stares, sat down and casually turned toward Pete and said, "Who. Is. THAT?"

They all laughed.

"He asked the same thing about you." The ladies oohed and ahhed, but I waved them off so I could get the full skinny on this handsome stranger.

Pete leaned in, chin resting on folded hands. "I honestly don't know tons about him, but if you're okay with it, I'll give him your cell number and have him reach out to you. I think he goes to church."

I had made it clear to my co-workers that I desired a man who loved the Lord. I had even shared with a few that I was celibate. Pete knew that his friend having a church home was code for: he just might be your type.

Trying to play it cool, I nodded while Pete pulled out his phone. Inside, though? Let's just say if pelvic pumps were a language, I was fluent.

Sexy? Check.
Athletic? Check.
Taller than me in heels? Check.
Goes to church? Possible check.

That possible check was enough for me to respond to the text I quickly received from Pete's friend, Kissing Kevin. When my phone vibrated against the desk, Pete peeked over the cubicle. "That better be him. I told him to text you now."

Kissing Kevin didn't waste time. He mentioned that he saw my smile and immediately wanted to get to know me better.

Recognizes my fineness? Check.

We quickly made plans to get together for dinner in the next few days. Until then, we kept a steady flow of conversation. He told me about why he was looking for a new job. He had served on the police force but was now seeking a different path. He also admitted that he'd been married before—but due to his own infidelity, the marriage ended in divorce.

Honest and recognized his own faults? Check.

Our first date was at a hip restaurant with an artsy atmosphere and unique dishes. When I walked in, he was easy to spot because he stood head and shoulders above the others. Judging by the look on his face, he was definitely happy to see me.

"You're breathtaking," he whispered as we hugged hello.

Knows how to give a good compliment? Check.

I ordered a Diet Coke, and he ordered a cocktail. Then he asked, "Are you sure that's all you want?"

"Mmm-hmm," I responded, bracing myself for the barrage of questions that were sure to follow. Whenever I didn't drink, it was normally a discussion, be it from friends, colleagues, or dates. Some were appalled, others were just curious. But for me, clarity mattered. I could think sharper without alcohol, and that was imperative for a first date when I needed to, and I properly assessed the man sitting across from me.

"Okay," he shrugged. "I'm so hungry. What we should get. Any recommendations?"

Not tripping on me not drinking? Double check.

Kissing Kevin had a hearty appetite for all things. Over appetizers and dinner, he shared more of his story. He was biracial with Black and Asian. His grandmother was the matriarch of his family and they had a close relationship. His brother was a choir director in a local church. His parents were still married.

This was my opening. As a certified church girl who was looking for a man with his own relationship with Christ, I leaned into the topic.

"Oh, do you go to the same church your brother goes to?"

"Me? Nah, church hasn't really been my thing. I know I should go, but I don't know." He shrugged and shifted his eyes toward the floor.

I softened my tone to convey compassion, not judgement, before probing deeper. "You don't know what?"

"I feel like I've done too much." I waited in silence. A skill I learned at work—if you sit in silence long enough, the other person will inevitably keep on talking. And talk he did. He shared that he didn't feel like he was worthy of good things happening in his life because of the bad things he had done in his past. He was hoping to make amends and start fresh.

Self-conscious about sharing too much, he quickly flipped the spotlight back on me. He asked about my professional journey, where I was from, how I liked living in NorCal versus SoCal and what my future aspirations were. Then, without fail, came the classic question every single woman knows too well:

"So why is someone as beautiful, put together, and amazing as you are still single?"

I hated being asked that question. Mainly because I didn't really know the answer. My relationship status wasn't something I was fully in control of. I had tried to take control before and learned the hard way that managing my own love life was not my strength. But knowing that didn't mean I stopped asking God the same question—just in a whiny, complaining tone when I was tired of waiting. I would remind God (as if He didn't know) that I was intelligent, ambitious, attractive and fun—qualities of a good woman. I'd list my loving family, my solid friendships, my high emotional IQ, and my self-awareness. Surely these were valuable traits, were they not?

While I didn't know why I was still single, I'd been asked often enough to have a reasonable response ready for Kissing Kevin.

"Thank you. I appreciate the compliment. I would be lying to say I haven't asked myself the same thing. But ultimately, I've given control of my love life to God and therefore, am no longer dating just to date. I also am not having sex before marriage, which is very different for me but important, nonetheless. I understand how that decision changes my dating pool pretty drastically. But I believe God will bring the right option along in His time." I smiled and Kissing Kevin smiled back.

"You're even more amazing than I thought," he said. Inside, I was just glad that he didn't immediately ask for the check.

Cool with my celibacy? *Heeeey*. Check, check and check again.

Our dinner ended too soon, and Kissing Kevin walked me to my car. He gave me a warm hug and said he would call me the next day.

And that he did. Our conversations grew, expanding into career experiences, fitness tips, and everyday life. Before long, we had plans for date number two.

We met at a mom-n-pop Mediterranean restaurant where the plates were hearty and one of my favorite ice cream shops was down the street.

I wore my hair curly instead of straight and when he saw me, he said, "I like it. You're beautiful as always. Now I feel like I can actually talk to you without being completely distracted."

I wasn't sure how to respond to that, so I didn't.

After dinner, we walked hand-in-hand to the ice cream shop. We stood in line, and he looked deep into my eyes and said, "I want to know everything about you."

Again, I wasn't sure how to respond. Instead, I blushed and looked away. It was too soon for everything. We were still only in the early stages, and part of me was on the fence about him based on what he shared about his ex-wife and his views on faith. I was doing my best not to judge too quickly and see him for who he was, not just who I wanted him to be. He had a habit of self-depreciating but something about it wasn't genuine. I needed more time to observe. Plus, it was only our second date.

After we got our ice cream, we stole an empty seat in the corner. He asked about the faint scar under my right eyebrow. At first, I wasn't sure what scar he was referring to, but then I recalled a cheerleading incident from high school.

As I talked, he scooted closer. He devoured his ice cream in a matter of minutes while I was still savoring mine.

"Your lips are so beautiful," he said, licking his own.

I flirtatiously responded, "They're soft too."

"Oh really?" he said leaning in.

Our lips touched and my body felt a jolt below the belt. Judging by his response, he felt it too. Conscious that we were still in an ice cream shop, I quickly pulled back.

"Wow. That was better than I had even imagined," he said, leaning in closer.

I hadn't kissed anyone in what felt like forever, so I was still processing what I was feeling. It was soft, sensual even. I wanted to do it again, but I didn't trust myself. I was only a couple years into my celibacy journey and wasn't sure if my resolve was rooted in a true desire to honor God, or if I had just managed to avoid temptation because I hadn't met anyone I found attractive enough to test me. I would like to believe it was about honoring God, but I don't think I was there just yet. I wore my celibacy like a piece of chunky armor at the time. *(Chastity belts didn't have nothing on me.)*

Kissing Kevin walked me to my car and before we parted ways, we gave that ice cream shop kiss a fuller expression. This time his hands roamed more than I expected, but I didn't stop him.

He kept asking me out, and I kept saying yes. Each time became steamier than the last. Our attraction became a running topic of conversation, and like clockwork—once the sun went down, the heat turned up. I didn't object right away because I liked the attention. After all, it was catering to a part of my desires that hadn't received much attention over the last couple of years. Then came the texts. His "goodnight" messages soon included pictures of himself provocatively posed—sometimes with nothing but a towel, other times with his shorts hanging way too low.

The first time he sent a sexy picture over text, I was taken aback. It's cringy for a guy to send unsolicited sexy pics and I prayed that he wasn't about to send a picture of his private member. I heard about how common that was in dating *(Note to the fellas: those pics get shared with her friends and nine times out of ten, women are cracking jokes at your expense.)* I also hoped he wasn't expecting the same type of picture in return.

Also, when I compared the pictures to the man standing in front of me, I realized that something was off. In his photos he had a defined six-pack and chiseled arms. In person, while muscular, the six-pack looked more like a dessert-induced gut and his arms had lost some of their definition. He was easily carrying an extra thirty pounds or so on his frame. I didn't think much of it because I was still attracted to him, but it did feel odd that he sent sexy pictures from a different time in his life.

Our in-person encounters had stayed PG (slowly leaning more toward PG-13) but rated R was around the corner. One night, he sent me a more explicit text that made my eyebrows shoot up to my hairline. Things were officially about to get out of hand if I didn't step in and redirect where this was headed.

Here is the thing, I knew exactly what I needed to say. But I also knew those words contradicted my desires. The truth? I wanted to do exactly what he was suggesting, but I told God I wasn't going to do that with anyone other than my husband.

Paul described this tension perfectly in Romans 7:15. I don't know if he was dealing with sexual temptation from a person he was completely attracted to, but he did write about knowing what you should do while wanting to do the exact opposite. Paul gets me.

But Paul also said that nothing good comes from giving into what the flesh craves. Just because it would feel good didn't mean it was good for you.

I let the Holy Spirit do what only He could do. I fought against the urge to tell him to "come over" and instead chose obedience. I told him clearly that while I did find him attractive, I was committed to not having sex before marriage. I asked him to respect my boundaries—or let me know if this wasn't something he wanted to continue.

Like a true gentleman, he immediately apologized and promised not to steer our conversation down that road again. He layered on a few more compliments about how irresistibly beautiful he found me and assured me he would "find a way to manage his desires." With that, we shifted the conversation to other topics.

A few weeks later, I made the decision to let him hang out at my house. Having a man come over to my house was a big, big deal. For one, I've always been particular about who I allow in my personal space, especially a man I'm dating. Second, I hadn't even invited new friends to my house yet because hospitality was not my strong suit. I would forget to offer water or a snack and would worry about people enjoying themselves. And third, I wasn't sure if I trusted myself around him . . . alone, behind closed doors.

There was a dent in my armor.

When the day came, the old Carrie—full of her sexy, party girl ways—was itching to show up and show out. She wanted to act on everything Kissing Kevin had slyly mentioned in his texts. But the new Carrie, the one who had submitted her life to Jesus, wanted to keep him at a distance. She knew it was the right thing to do, not only to honor God but also protect her heart from getting too attached to someone when there was no commitment or talk of a real future together.

I almost called him and canceled. As I nervously cleaned and paced around my apartment I was hoping he would cancel on me instead. He was running late and parking at my place was always a nightmare, so maybe frustration would send him home. While I waited for him to arrive, my thoughts spiraled. *Did I even like him? What did we have in common? Did I really want to date a guy who sent fake sexy pictures? Something about that wasn't right. Who does that? And what about his views on Jesus and Christianity? Did he even have a point of view? What fruit had I witnessed?* He seemed to be finding himself and trying to adhere to my guidelines versus understanding why I set these standards and what that obedience meant to God.

While I listed everything I didn't like about him, my craving for attention silenced my questions and reassured me that it was harmless. It was just a simple movie night. We would watch tv, maybe kiss a little, and that would be it.

Before I could continue down a self-induced path of anxiety, Kissing Kevin arrived at my door with food in his hand and a smile on his face. He wore gray shorts and a too-tight t-shirt, a light sheen of sweat glistening from his trek up to my apartment. I slid open my patio door to let in a breeze, but his presence filled my tiny one-bedroom more than I anticipated.

Complimentary as always, he commented on how nice and clean my place was and how I was such a boss to be able to afford my own spot in such an affluent area. Then he laughed at my attempt to be cozy casual. When we went out, I was always in heels and a dress or fashion-forward outfit. Tonight, in order to keep it low-key, I wore oversized sweatpants and a basic t-shirt. He called it cozy casual; I called it a strategic attempt to look as unappealing as possible.

After eating, we snuggled up in my oversized chair, settling in for the movie. Before the opening scene was complete, his hand was up my shirt, and his lips were a fast follow. I felt his body responding and mine wasn't far behind.

I had made up my mind that I was not going down that road, but just as I pulled back to tell him we needed to slow down, he pulled his shorts down.

I froze.

An internal battle ensued. I wanted to do everything I knew to do with what I saw in front of me. It was there. And so was I.

But what surprised me most was the fury that rose up inside me. Furious was the only word that came close to capturing the mess of emotions firing all at once: desire, torn, nervous, annoyed, shocked, excited, and angry. Angry because I knew too much. I knew what happens when you let lust drive your choices. I knew the aftermath of crossing boundaries, the confusion, the guilt, the emptiness.

Angry because I had been clear about what was not going to happen that night, and yet here I was—backed into a moment I had prayed to avoid. I was nervous. How was I going to tell this man to put his penis back in his pants when the very sight of it made my body hum?

I wasn't worried about him, although in hindsight, I realize this could have been a dangerous situation as a woman a third of his size. I was worried about me. I was worried that I was going to go back down a path that God had healed me from. Walking down the road of sexual lust wasn't what He had for me.

I stood up, backed away, and yelled for him to "put it away!"

"What?" He smirked, almost amused, like he knew what he was doing.

"Listen, you and I both know what you're doing. Put it up. I told you that's not going down. Put it away!" I walked into the kitchen just to get some space and breathe. My mind raced—should I kick him out completely or just try to salvage the night?

"I'm sorry, Carrie." He came over to me. "That was too much too soon. I get it. My bad."

I didn't know how to respond. Yes, it was too much, but my mind kept replaying all the moments that led up to this—every date where his hands wandered, every kiss that lingered too long. He started to flirtatiously console me. I backed away, but he followed. I playfully ran to the entryway, and he ran right after me. For a few minutes we danced this playful game, but with every step, my defenses weakened. My body betrayed me. The flame of desire flared hot again.

And just like that—I was back to square one.

The possibility of sex was tugging at my oversized sweatpants when it hit me: I had not set myself up for success for that night.

Every woman makes an important decision before a date—what underwear is she going to wear. Believe it or not, that choice often determines the type of night she's preparing for. Sexy underwear can be empowering and confidence-building, but it can also be tempting because part of you hopes someone will see it.

As a woman practicing celibacy, my underwear drawer presented me with options that were less fashion and more foresight. My first choice was ol' faithful granny panties. You know the ones. Full-bottom coverage, 100% cotton, soft as butter, and in your drawer longer than you care to admit. They stay put, they never give you a wedgie, and they scream, "This night is going absolutely nowhere." But they're also the pair you'd never let anyone outside of your mom (*if her*) see you in them because they are unflattering in every way. *Yes, those granny panties.*

My second choice was the red lacy thong. Some women wear thongs every day. I am not that woman. If I put on a lace thong, it's because I expect someone to see it. Nothing about them are comfortable to me, and I always feel weird pulling them back up after I have gone to the bathroom. In my world, a thong wasn't a practical choice; it was a signal. Choosing anything remotely similar to the lacy thong would have brought CeeLo Green's, hip hop artist from Atlanta, words to life, "She knew she was going to perform before she came."

Deciding which undies to put on is just like the process that begins when deciding to sin. First comes the thought. The thought takes root based on a fleshly desire that is already there. As my Pastor has said many times, it's only temptation because you want to do it. Temptation must be squashed in the thought phase. Otherwise, the door is open for sin to enter and have its way.

Choosing granny panties before a date wasn't just about what I wore under clothes. It represented preparing myself to pursue God in the face of temptation. It was the equivalent of choosing Christ and dying to your flesh. Resisting the urge to slip into the lacy thong signified my decision to set myself up for obedience, not sin.

But my choice that night left the door ajar.

Instead of putting on my full-coverage, non-sexy, borderline embarrassing granny panties, I put on my "we'll see where this goes panties." They were cute and flirty and willing to be taken off if necessary. I hadn't shut the door early enough.

But then, by what I can only describe as a complete miracle, I stopped. I backed away and asked Kissing Kevin to leave. He balked for a second but then left quietly, without the usual promise to call or text later.

I locked my door and let out the breath I didn't realize I'd been holding. Relief washed over me. Relief that I hadn't tied myself emotionally, spiritually, or physically to this man. But it also sent me into some heavy self-reflection.

Because while it looked like willpower, it wasn't. It was the Holy Spirit giving me courage to resist. I knew too well what happens when you let lust call the shots—how it entangles you, clouds your judgment, and leaves you emptier than before. God knew it too, and He protected me despite myself.

My father always quoted the scripture, "Can a man take fire into his bosom and not be burned?" (Proverbs 6:27) No, he cannot. I had chances to put out the fire again and again. Instead, I blew air into the flames until they went from smoldering to blazing hot. Then I invited it into my home, wearing my "we'll see where this goes" panties. I was practically asking for a third-degree burn.

When I decided to date, I had good intentions. I told men about my boundaries and about how I love the Lord. But if my actions didn't match my words, how could I have expected anyone else to honor boundaries I wasn't truly living out myself? Please know, I'm not excusing his behavior or giving him permission to ignore my no. He was responsible for his choices, but he only did what I allowed.

It started with flattery. Looking back, the compliments would ramp up whenever I put boundaries in place. It was a form of manipulation, but I welcomed it because it fed my flesh in the moment. I wanted to be desired. I wanted to be taken out on dates. I wanted to feel a connection with someone because it had been so long since I felt that way. Kissing Kevin spoke to my flesh at a time when my flesh was doing most of the talking. By feeding those desires instead of strengthening my spirit, I blinded myself to the tactics designed to make me compromise.

The thing is, we never connected on anything that mattered. Our conversations were rather surface, and we didn't have that much in common. He wasn't someone I wanted as a friend, let alone a potential partner. He was just a distraction—nice to look at, easy to spend time with, but ultimately in need of healing himself, just like me.

And that was the real lesson. This whole situation showed me I wasn't ready to date. I couldn't value someone else's heart when I was too busy trying to guard and protect my own. Out of fear of being hurt or wasting time, I kept trying to snatch back the pen I had given to the Author of my love story.

Holy Spirit!!

You betta' be out here in these streets keeping a sista's foot from getting caught in a trap! Whew. Thank You for helping me dodge that bullet. Can you imagine how devastated I would have felt had I slept with Kissing Kevin only to have his ex-wife already coming back in the picture? Sigh. Thank you for removing unnecessary drama.

Lord, I know I pray about getting married a lot, but perhaps I need to focus on finding contentment in my single season. These folks are out here wildin'. As hard as this solitary life can be, I know you are keeping me.

I must also say sorry. I have been using my celibacy as a defense mechanism at times instead of relying on you to sustain and guide me. This whole no sex at all thing while dating still feels new. I'm figuring out how to manage this and the emotions that come along with it. Will it ever get easier?

What was that? I think I hear you telling me to stop leaning on my own understanding and trying to figure things out? You want me to trust you and bring everything before you . . . even sexual desires? Oh, okay. Got it.

Can I ask one more thing? Lord, am I the hold up? I feel like I keep learning lessons in this journey. But what are you working out of me to prepare me for this next step of life?

Chapter 13

Am I The Drama?

In some sermons for singles waiting on their future spouse, I've heard it taught that God may have you waiting on your spouse because either you're not ready, God is readying the circumstances, or He is readying your spouse.

There is always a reason for a waiting season. Since mine felt particularly prolonged, I asked God, *Is it me? Am I the drama?* I needed to know if He was waiting on me to change or learn whatever lesson He was trying to teach me.

My waiting season reminded me of the Israelites. Their journey to the Promised Land could have taken eleven days. Instead, it took forty years.

Let that sink in.

Eleven days versus forty years.

I don't know about you, but I never want to spend years learning a lesson I could have learned in days. However, God, in His sovereignty, knew the Israelites better than they knew themselves. He knew that if they took the direct route, they would have been easily discouraged. He also knew they needed to get the "Egypt" out of their system prior to entering the Promised Land.

And if I'm honest, my single season looked a lot like their wilderness. I wasn't just waiting; I was wandering. I wrestled with disobedience. I grumbled. I complained. I idolized relationships. I got greedy for attention. And all the while, God was patiently working the "Egypt" out of me—teaching me how to value His promises without dragging my old baggage with me. After my colorful dating experiences, I thought I was ready. I resisted the temptation to compromise my faith with Academic Aaron. I learned the power of purposeful preparation with Kissing Kevin. I even ended the back-and-forth dance with Entertaining Eddie. What else could God possibly require?

I didn't want to create the illusion that I was this perfect Proverbs 31 woman. Nor was every man the villain. Nope. Not at all.

In my desire to find a new boo or simply gratify my fleshly desires, I stepped on a few toes and misrepresented God in more ways than one. I also dated with an unhealed heart. And when you date with an unhealed heart, you don't just hurt yourself, you usually take someone else down with you. One in particular, let's call him Gentle Gerry, stands out.

Let me start from the beginning.

"You have a very distinct presence."

I turned around to see where the deep baritone came from. Standing there was a guy towering over me, even in my four-inch heels. He was easily six-foot-three or taller. He had a deep chocolate complexion dotted with miniature moles, along with thin dreads tipped with blonde all over his head. He naturally stood a bit hunched over as if he was used to shrinking himself in the presence of others or ducking under shortened doorways.

"Thank you. That's a beautiful compliment," I replied.

He shrugged and let a sheepish grin spread across his face. He struggled to look me in my eyes.

"I don't think we have met before. I'm Carrie." I held out my hand. I normally recognized most of the Black people in my office but had never noticed him before. I figured he was new to the company. Turns out, Gentle Gerry wasn't as new as I thought.

"I've seen you before. You always look so fashionable and ..." his eyes shifted downward, "confident."

"Thanks. I really appreciate that." I smiled. That was a pleasant boost to my morning. "I'm sure I'll see you around." I waved as I went to pay for my breakfast and start my workday.

A few weeks later, I received an instant message on my laptop in the middle of a meeting.

"Hi Carrie, do you have a sec to chat?"

I didn't recognize the name and since I was trying to stay focused, I minimized the message and planned to respond later.

Hours passed before I pulled the message back up. Still no profile picture. Still no recognition of the name. I typed a quick, *Hi there*, waiting to see what this "business partner" needed. "Oh, I'm glad you responded. I thought I might have messaged the wrong person."

I waited for the person to type more.

"How is your day going?"

"It's good. Just busy." I was politely trying to encourage the messenger to get to the point.

"I don't know if you remember me, but I've been trying to get in contact with you since I met you in the cafeteria."

I searched my brain and couldn't remember who I had recently met in the café. There were thousands of employees in the building, and it was common for me to interact with quite a few of them on any given day.

The messenger referenced himself as the tall Black guy with dreads and my lightbulb lit up. Gentle Gerry! My tone softened. I adjusted my responses to be friendly instead of curt. He kept asking simple questions, and eventually it became clear—he wasn't messaging about work. He was reaching out to ask me on a date.

Unbeknownst to me, after our first cafeteria encounter, he had spent weeks combing the company intranet, hoping to find my last name and a way to contact me. Too shy to approach me again in person, he worked quietly behind the scenes. One of his team members even egged him on every morning with, "Did you see her today?" They would brainstorm ways for him to casually bump into me—or what he would say if he finally got the chance.

Eventually, his search turned up an outdated company application where he found a five-year-old photo of me. That was his window in.

I was genuinely surprised and quite flattered that he was that pressed to track me down and ask me out. Gentle Gerry was incredibly shy, but there was something disarmingly open and sincere about his intentions. I said yes.

For our first date, we went to one of the area's top young professional hangouts—a hip sushi restaurant that was dimly lit with red-tinted lanterns casting a warm glow over mahogany tables. Chopsticks rested neatly on decorative stones, and shoji screens divided the sections of the room. A low baseline vibrated through the speakers as the host guided us to our table. I could tell he was nervous. He fidgeted with his shirt, and tucked his chin when he answered questions. I leaned into my natural charm, laughing easily and offering plenty of smiles to put him at ease.

Once he found his footing, Gentle Gerry didn't hesitate to go deep. He laid his cards on the table. He had joint custody of twin biracial girls, Black and Asian. And his greatest hope was that they would embrace their identity as Black women. What weighed on him was his strained relationship with their mother, whom he described as selfish and not particularly maternal.

Whenever a guy doesn't have positive things to say about the mother of his kids, my senses go on high alert. First, I realize that I'm only hearing one side of the story. It takes two to tango and no one is perfect. Second, I try to discern if he's speaking through the microphone of unforgiveness or an unhealed heart. And lastly, a strained relationship with a child's mother normally equates to Baby Momma Drama. That drama can show up in all kinds of ways—financially, emotionally, or physically.

My alert was warranted. As we talked more, Gentle Gerry shared how the mother of his daughters cheated on him and abruptly ended the relationship. In the aftermath, he had spiraled into a bout of depression—one he admitted he was still recovering from.

Just as the mood settled into that somber honesty, a man walked up to our table. He stood right beside us, eyes trained only on me. His face was familiar, but I couldn't place him. "Hey girl, how you been?" He stood at the side of our table, facing me but never acknowledged Gentle Gerry.

"Uh, I'm goooood?" I raised my eyebrows to indicate that I did not remember his name.

"So, I see. You look good, real good." While I couldn't remember his name, I immediately recognized his pinky ring and how we had met. Months earlier, I was having lunch alone at a restaurant in a completely different part of the city. He was there with his friend, and they struck up a conversation with me. He was considerably older, but friendly and personable. We shared some laughs and small talk, then he and his friend covered my lunch tab. He oozed with confidence, but even then, something about him felt . . . off. Behind his smile, there lingered a hint of creepiness I couldn't shake. I thanked them for covering my lunch and left without a second thought. We never exchanged numbers.

So why he felt compelled to interrupt my conversation with Gentle Gerry that night, I had no idea. His cockiness and complete disregard for Gentle Gerry's presence were unacceptable. Just as I was about to dismiss him, Gentle Gerry responded with, "She does, doesn't she?"

The Swaggy Stranger turned slightly toward him, and I took the opportunity to introduce Gentle Gerry, who made it clear we were enjoying our dinner and wanted to get back to it. Thankfully, he took the hint and backed off. I was embarrassed but I'll admit, my ego was a little inflated. I had never experienced anything like that before. Awkward as it was, it played out okay.

"Sorry about that," I said, unsure how Gerry would react, especially considering the raw story he had just been sharing with me. "It's okay. You're a beautiful woman. I assume you have several guys vying for your attention."

I didn't. Not even one. My phone was drier than the Sahara, but I didn't want to tell him that. I liked the idea of him thinking I was a hot commodity. I simply shrugged, feigned humility, and smiled before asking him to continue with his story.

As he talked, I took the opportunity to really study him. There was a heaviness about him, a sadness that seemed to dim even his rich brown skin. His smile never quite reached his eyes. His lips were darker, the telltale sign of someone who smoked too much, and his shoulders slumped as if weighed down by burdens too heavy to carry. Even though we worked for an apparel retailer, fashion clearly wasn't on his priority list. His oversized clothes looked more like camouflage, a way to disappear rather than be seen. The faded black shirt and equally worn pants gave off a 90's vibe that felt stuck in time.

As the night continued, Gentle Gerry opened up about what he was looking for. He longed for a relationship again—the comfort, the affection, the love of a woman. He held romantic connections in high regard but now, with two daughters, he was careful. He wanted someone who could be a good role model to them, someone who could show his girls what a functional, healthy relationship looked like—something they couldn't witness in their parents' strained dynamic.

It was rare for a man to speak so openly and earnestly about his feelings. Refreshing, yes—but also concerning. The way he spoke, I couldn't shake the sense that what he really craved was relief from the loneliness that had grown uncontrollably in the years since his breakup.

So, I asked about his faith. He called his faith an "exploratory journey." Curious, I asked him to explain what he meant. Gentle Gerry said he was familiar with Christianity, but he'd also studied other religions, searching for the peace and joy he desperately wanted.

I shared about my church, how it focuses on holy living, and how much it has blessed me since I moved to the Bay Area during a season of heartbreak. In response, he asked if he could attend with me.

Now, some ladies might be excited at this response. But I was wary. For one, it was clear Gentle Gerry had no relationship of his own with Christ. I worried his desire to come wasn't about Jesus at all, but about me.

For two, everyone knows that when a single woman brings a man to church, people automatically assume that they are together, together. And selfishly, I didn't want to deter any man who might have had his eye on me from shooting his shot simply because he saw me there with someone else. And finally, practicality. We already worked at the same company (even though we rarely saw one another) so did I really want to also be linked to him at church?

Whether you've dated a lot or a little, at some point during the date, a woman sizes things up. She wonders if she can see herself kissing him or being romantically involved. Sometimes this happens during a date, sometimes in a casual interaction with a cute guy who has potential. For me, it took all of fifteen minutes to realize I couldn't see myself kissing Gentle Gerry. The attraction just wasn't there. But he looked at me like I was the most radiant thing in the room, and honestly . . . I was bored. So,

I told myself I could at least help with his wardrobe and have a little fun along the way.

Let's pause the story here. You're probably thinking—*Carrie, you did exactly what we're not supposed to do. You wasted that man's time, knowing from the jump you weren't into him.*

And you'd be right. Every part of that is true. I knew better. But like I've said, this dating journey is about sharing all of it—the good, the bad, and the messy. I wanted to be transparent about the areas where I had opportunities to grow. My actions here were selfish. Not all desires in singleness are sexual—sometimes it's just the desire to be admired, desired, or distracted. Since my dating season wasn't unfolding how I'd hoped, I resorted to habits that were self-centered and, in the end, hurtful.

Back to the story.

Between our first and second dates, we talked often. That's when I learned more about Gently Gerry. I learned that he was a smoker who smoked more than cigarettes. He struggled with insomnia and used weed to ease his anxiety. His odd sleep patterns explained the weary look on his face—and also why I often woke up to text messages he had sent in the middle of the night.

He was a deep thinker and often shared long, introspective thoughts with me. He'd even started to crack open his Bible and ask a few questions. I encouraged him to get more active—work out, eat healthier—because those things affect how you feel about yourself. The more we talked, the more I noticed small shifts. He laughed a little more. When we grabbed coffee midweek or crossed paths in the office, his countenance seemed lighter, even brighter.

Date number two included eating and shopping. Gentle Gerry was quite the foodie and loved exposing me to unique restaurants that specialized in farm-to-table menus. He was at his most confident when discussing food or various recipes; his smile finally reached his eyes when he described new flavors or places he wanted to try. Ironically, he rarely cooked for himself or his daughters, but he knew every top spot for ramen, sushi, and even the best pizza in town.

He asked for my fashionista expertise in reviving his wardrobe, which I happily obliged. Shopping was one of my favorite pastimes, and styling people to bring out their inner confidence was the reward. Gentle Gerry's inner confidence was hiding a bit deeper than I expected.

We walked into a popular retailer known for its classic style, and I handed him a selection of basics—nothing too trendy, just some clean pieces that could bring life into his closet. But once he was in the fitting room, he didn't want to come out.

Yes, this forty-something, six-foot-something grown man whispered through the crack in the door about how he didn't want me to see his *moobs*[3]. At first I laughed because I thought he was joking. But then he shared that his daughters often teased him about them when they were lounging around the house, and it had made him deeply self-conscious. He had put on more weight over the last year, thanks to constant anxiety and inconsistent sleep.

"But I've been inspired by you and working out more, which I think helps, but I am still not going to show you my moobs," he said from inside the fitting room.

As I stood there, I thought about every self-deprecating comment he had ever made and the way his shoulders slumped

---

3   Moobs = man boobs (his word, not mine).

as if carrying invisible weight. I had mistaken it all for shyness, but this was a deeper sense of incompleteness and insecurity than I realized.

I softened my voice and reminded him that no body, his or mine, was perfect. I assured him I would never make him do anything he didn't want to do, but if he truly wanted my help, I needed to see the clothes on him. My goal wasn't to judge his body, I explained, but to help him feel good about what he saw in the mirror.

Still hesitant, we struck a compromise. He wouldn't come all the way out of the fitting room, but he let me peek my head inside. Even then, he avoided my eyes in the mirror as if embarrassed to meet them. I tried to break the ice with a smile and a compliment about how the color played on his chocolate brown complexion. The shirt itself was too tight, pulling in ways that weren't flattering. I reassured him it wasn't a reflection of him—just the wrong size and a poor choice on my part. I could almost see his shoulders relax as he exhaled, comforted by that truth.

By the end of the date, he had several new shirts and pants that brought his personal style into the current century. If I didn't know any better, he walked a bit taller with each store we left. His posture seemed lighter, almost as though every well-fitting outfit added a layer of confidence he had been missing.

At our last stop, while waiting for the salesperson to find his size, he turned to me and said, "You should find a pair too."

I laughed it off. "I have plenty of shoes. This trip is about you." "They're on me. I want to thank you for helping me out today."

I wasn't really used to men buying me things unless we were in a long-term relationship, and I was a bit out of practice on how to respond. On one hand, the army green suede lace-up ankle boots I'd admired earlier were calling my name. But on the other hand, accepting a gift from a man I wasn't truly attracted to, and had no intentions of dating long term, felt uncomfortably misleading.

I had friends and had heard stories about women who let men but them things all the time. But for me, it didn't sit right. I already felt like I was dating Gentle Gerry for attention and a good meal—I didn't want to add expensive gifts to the list.

The fitting room incident didn't help. While I appreciated his vulnerability, I preferred a confident man, a man who felt good in his own skin and knew he was more than just good looks. I've dated a guy with moobs and an oversized belly, but his confidence filled the room so strongly that not one woman in the room was thinking twice about what some would consider flaws.

This kind of confidence is what I like to call "The Rick Ross Effect". Rick Ross, a hip-hop artist who raps about un-Christian-like things, may not be everyone's idea of universally attractive. He doesn't have a six-pack or a full head of hair. But you can't tell him he isn't the man of your dreams. His presence, confidence, big smile, and hustler mentality make him magnetic. The Rick Ross Effect gives you machismo at its peak (and I'm sure that comes with its own side of drama, but you get my point).

Gentle Gerry had the opposite of the Rick Ross Effect.

So when he offered to buy me the boots, I declined. He offered again. I would like to say he insisted, but it wasn't quite an insistent claim. He just said, "I won't keep asking. It's up to you."

I let him buy the boots, but it didn't sit well with me. In my head, I justified it as payment for my styling services, but deep down I knew I was using him—for meals, attention, and the chance to say I was dating someone whenever friends or coworkers inevitably asked. I didn't want to feel lame or undesirable. Saying I had "someone" in my life, even if he wasn't the right someone, gave me a false sense of validation.

My Pastor calls this the pride of optics: caring more about how others perceive you than how your behavior is seen by God. That was me. I was so concerned about what others thought, I was willing to misuse Gentle Gerry just to keep up appearances. I wanted people to know I wasn't sitting at home doing nothing on Friday and Saturday nights (even though that's exactly what I was doing)

This was not one of my best moments.

When I responded to those instant messages and remembered him from the café, I already knew he wasn't the kind of man I preferred to date. I also knew I could easily manipulate him or walk over his feelings if I chose to. That knowledge should have stopped me in my tracks. I had vowed not to date just to date. I wanted to be intentional, not wasting my own time or anyone else's money, energy, or emotions. When I made that vow, I didn't realize how many nights I would be sitting alone at home. And when I grew tired of those lonely nights, my judgment slipped.

I knew my personality could crush or encourage Gentle Gerry, and in reality, I did both. Part of me saw him as a cute little project. I would help get his wardrobe together and have some delicious meals in the process. But when he leaned in for affection or tried to cross the line into romance, I easily turned him down.

For the record, I think the young kids call these "toxic traits." *Sigh.*

Gentle Gerry asked again about joining me at church. By this time, we'd been on a handful of dates. My attraction to him hadn't shifted one bit. I finally told him I didn't mind if he came, but he needed to come for himself, not for me. If he showed up, we would drive separately and we would not sit together. I emphasized how important it was for him to have *his own* relationship with Jesus, because deep down, I knew I wasn't representing Jesus well. I had no interest in Evangelist Dating[4], and I didn't want him to associate Christianity with me and how I treated him. I also knew that the shelf life on our dating was about to expire.

He did end up coming to church. I did not see him during service but spotted him afterward in the lobby. I was standing with a close friend, so I gave a quick introduction before we headed off to brunch. My friend was none the wiser because I casually explained that he was a coworker who wanted to be more. As we sat at brunch, I realized I couldn't string Gentle Gerry along any longer. I could tell he wanted to be affectionate toward me, and I just didn't have it in me to fake attraction. Over the past few weeks, I learned that his depression and anxiety ran much deeper than what he initially shared. He revealed more about his coping behaviors outside of smoking and working, and I realized that he was categorizing me into his coping mechanisms—hence the desire to join me at church. He then began to

---

4   Evangelist Dating = when you try to get the person you're dating to give their life to Christ so you can keep dating them and claim you are equally yoked.

drop bigger hints that he wanted me to meet his girls, possibly do their hair or teach them about how to be confident women.

Danger! Danger! Abort the mission.

It's one thing to toy with the feelings of a grown man, but I was certainly not about to do that with young, innocent little girls. The problem was, I didn't know how to cut things off without creating an incredibly awkward situation. We worked in the same building, and since we'd started dating, I regularly saw his large shoulders and blonde-tipped twists in the morning crowd, café, and elevator banks. Add to that his own history of volatile conflicts with women and family, and I worried about what an ending might trigger in him.

But then, the choice started making itself. Soon after our brunch date, Gentle Gerry started going dark and his communication with me became more erratic. At first, he would just stop responding for half the day and into the night, and I would wake up in the morning with a text stating how he smoked, fell asleep, and was knocked out for the remainder of the night. Other times, when he had his daughters, he'd go silent without explanation, only to reappear later with a casual "when I'm with my girls, nothing else matters." Occasionally, he'd apologize and admit it was a "hard night," but the pattern continued.

I saw my opening.

The last time he went dark, he resurfaced with a single message. I didn't respond.

And that was the end of dating Gentle Gerry.

You may be thinking I ghosted him. *Not really.* By this point, his ghosting had become so frequent—I am pretty sure he lost interest or found a new interest elsewhere. *At least, this is what I tell myself.* I'm not really sure what happened. I'm just glad it did.

Still, I had to repent for using him. I knew all along that continuing to see him was disobedience. My intentions were selfish. I always said that if I ever had a conversation with him, I'd apologize.

I eventually had my chance.

Since the Bay Area is smaller than most people imagine, I ran into Gentle Gerry again. I was out with friends at a cute local restaurant that played hits from the 80s and 90s, and I needed to move a chair from the bar over to our table. When I turned around, he was standing right there.

His dreads were longer, and he looked a bit leaner. His complexion was brighter, and there was a lighter countenance about him. He still stooped a bit, as if trying to shrink the space he occupied, since he stood a head above most of the people in the room.

"Oh. Hi," was all I could say before quickly maneuvering around him with the chair. I sat with my friends and didn't turn to get another look until enough time had passed. He looked like he was with friends, and I think I even saw him laugh once or twice. I decided to keep my apology to myself. It was really for my benefit anyway.

Often in this dating journey, I've wondered: *Is it me? Am I the drama?* In this case, yes—I was the drama. God does not require perfection, but He is perfecting me. Each encounter, each mistake, each misstep is another place where He refines me—to do better, be better, give better—for the sake of His kingdom. And that, above all else, is the goal.

Lord . . . you know.

Chapter 14

Cuffing Season, Bad Advice, and Leftover Chicken Wings

I once wore flat shoes on a first date.

I know that doesn't sound like earth-shattering information, but for a woman such as myself who loves a good heel—especially a black strappy one—it was a *huge* deal.

Let me explain.

In climbing the corporate ladder and hitting my career goals, I noticed an unspoken reality: for many professional single women, there's a high chance you'll out-earn your future spouse. I've known several leaders who are the primary breadwinners while their husbands either stay home with the kids or make less.

This is often celebrated—until those same women enter the dating scene. Suddenly, it becomes an intimidation issue or an emasculation problem for select men. The woman is labeled "aggressive" instead of ambitious, or "difficult" instead of confident. There is also a false narrative that professionally successful women can't submit to a man or don't see the value in marriage.

Not to mention, women are also told they need to soften up, not be so confident—all so a guy will feel she is more approachable.

I wish I were making this up, y'all.

Most people didn't say these things directly, but the message slipped through in subtler ways. I once had a husband and wife tell me about their friend whom they thought I should meet. Before they shared his contact information, they lowered their voices, leaned in conspiratorially and said, "Every guy is not ready for a strong, confident woman. So just be conscious of that before you talk."

Excuse me? Why are you even introducing me to this kind of person?

In the beginning, I would listen to other well-meaning couples offering pointless advice about how to not come across as too driven, ambitious, or competent. I'd give them a blank stare in return. Internally, I had no idea how to respond. They were basically asking me not to be myself so a man would like me more.

Over time, the comments about how a man wanted a "soft woman" (implying I wasn't) started to weigh on me. I found myself trying to prove that I wasn't close-minded, too picky, or elitist about the men I dated. I was just looking for someone who loved Jesus, had a touch of gangsta, was attractive, and had a job. If he had muscles and a beard to go along with that, even better. I could figure out the rest later.

One night, some acquaintances and I grabbed dinner at a new hipster restaurant in town. It was one of those places with brick walls, high, exposed ceilings, and a garage door with a patio. It had a rustic, urban feel. It was a busy Friday night, but thankfully, we had reservations.

Two of us arrived at the same time and walked up to the hostess stand, where we were greeted by a guy who would make you do a double-take. He was tall with a full, luscious beard as black as coal. It was in stark contrast to his lighter skin tone. He also had a head full of curls that were the perfect mix of wild and perfectly coiled. His smile revealed straight white teeth with full lips, and it was so contagious you couldn't help but return it. Watching him interact with customers, it was clear his personality matched the warmth of his smile.

Once we were seated, he found reasons to stop by our table again and again—even though he wasn't frequenting anyone else's. I made a few attempts at flirting (*because sometimes, you just got to see if you've still got it*). My friends teased me because they hadn't seen me be interested enough in a guy to be flirtatious. I commented on how cute I thought he was and how I liked his style.

One of the ladies, Jen, lived in the neighboring building and often walked her dog by the restaurant. She shared that she'd chatted with him before. Jen's a bit more forward with her approach with men and rolled her eyes at my "antiquated" attempt at flirting. "Why don't you just say something to him?" she teased.

I explained my philosophy: I'll flirt, drop hints, and give a man the green light, but I wasn't about to ask a guy out. Nope. Not happening. Call me old-fashioned, call me stubborn, but I'd been down that road before, and let's just say the story isn't even worth sharing. B*uh-lieve me.*

In my mind, when grown men want something, they go after it. A job. A goal. Or yes, a woman. Fear of rejection is real, sure, but confidence is non-negotiable for me. If he couldn't find a way to approach me, or at least catch the ball if I threw it—that said something about his character. It wasn't compatible with mine.

"Would you go out with him?" one of the other ladies, Clarice, said.

"Yeah, why not?" I responded.

"I'm surprised. He's a bit more... well, let's say *rough around the edges* than what I would see you with." This was my sweet, demure friend's way of saying that she didn't see my dating someone who was working at a restaurant.

"You never know. He could own the restaurant. Or he could be the general manager or something," I responded.

"Working the hostess stand?" Clarice tilted her head to the right and squinted her eyes toward me.

"Aye, you gotta start somewhere, right? Or maybe somebody called out and he's covering their shift."

"I think it's cute that Carrie's attracted to him," Riley chimed in. She and I were the closest of the group, co-workers who had become genuine friends. Riley knew how rare it was for me to openly flirt and also knew I would never ask a man out on a date.

"Thank you, Riley. I know how to diversify my dating portfolio."

"Do you, though?" Jen asked. "Carrie, you have a type."

I found this almost laughable, considering Jen hadn't known me long enough to come to that conclusion. My expression must have given me away, because she quickly followed up with, "I mean, maybe I just see you as the type to only want a powerful man in a suit or at the top of his field. You will be the next power couple."

This wasn't the first time that I had heard this. People often assumed they knew the kind of man I'd be willing to date based on my demeanor or professional goals. But the way Jen positioned it, I don't think she meant it as a compliment.

"Are you telling me that you don't think I would date a man who is not in corporate America?" I asked.

"Oh, you're not that close-minded," she said. "I'm just saying he has to be a certain caliber."

"Listen, I just want someone who has a strong relationship with the Lord and a strong work ethic. You can be the garbage man but is that all you want? Do you want to one day own the garbage truck company or something?"

"That's just it!" Jen pointed my way. "Why can't him being a garbage man be enough for you?"

"How many men do you know dream of being a garbage man?" Riley countered.

"Exactly!" It was my turn to point. "Now, there are always reasons for why people do what they do or are at a certain point in life, but I want to build with someone. You can't build with someone who doesn't have a solid foundation."

The whole exchange reminded me of an iconic scene from the hit 90s sitcom, *A Different World*. Whitley, the southern belle, told Dwayne Wayne that she wanted a man who was "educated, enterprising, and ambitious."

When he asked, "So you wouldn't mind if he was poor?" she replied, "That type of man is never poor."

That's it. That's what I wanted Jen to understand.

Yes, being equally yoked spiritually matters, but I also believe a couple contemplating marriage should be equally yoked in ambition. One person can't be shooting for the stars while the other is lying in the grass, not even holding the bow. It's far easier to be pulled down than to pull someone up. Don't get me wrong, both people don't need to be dreamers. Every kite still needs a string.

"You just come across so put together," Jen said.

"You say that like it's a bad thing." I realized that to her, it was. She was saying what I heard so many others insinuate: because I carry myself a certain way, I wasn't approachable, or that's why men didn't like me.

We left the subject alone to discuss other life updates that didn't involve who I was willing to date.

A few days later, Jen texted me. She'd run into the host, Light-skin Leo, while walking her dog and casually told him I thought he was cute. Apparently, the feeling was mutual. She asked if she could give him my number. She had asked the initial screening questions and found out, "He's Christian and has a desire to own a restaurant." That was enough for me to give the go-ahead. Soon after, he texted, and we were scheduled to meet up by the end of the week.

Light-skin Leo was humorous, lively, and personable. Our brief conversations before our date were never short of loud bursts of laughter. I found myself looking forward to our time together.

Conscious of all the recent unsolicited advice I had received about not intimidating a man and the assumption that I'm not willing to date someone not in corporate America, I decided to try a different approach. Instead of giving him my normal glam, I switched my heeled boots out for flat, over-the-knee boots. I paired them with leggings, a denim shirt and a faux-fur vest. I gave casual chic at its finest.

About an hour before our date, he called and asked where I'd be coming from. When I told him my house, he asked me if I wanted to ride together. I politely declined and said I was just meet him there.

"Are you sure?" he asked.

For my safety, I would never let a guy know where I lived until we were much further along in the dating journey. Plus, he lived in the same area as the bar, so I wasn't sure if he was recommending that he pick me up or that I park at his house. Both were a "no" for me.

"Oh, my car isn't available right now, so I'm going to have to ride my bike. I was hoping you could pick me up instead." (Note: this was before sharing ride services were as popular as they are today.)

A man having a car was an absolute must for me. If we lived in New York or somewhere like that, maybe that would be permissible. But we lived in the Bay Area. Trains and buses could only do so much. Besides, what made him think I'd chauffeur him on our *first date?*

Trying not to assume the worst or come across as elitist, I offered to reschedule once he had his car back. I didn't want to inconvenience him, but I also was not going to pick him up.

"No, we can still meet tonight. I was just seeing if you could swoop me. I'll be there."

My expectations of the date were lowered immediately. I tried not to judge, but made a mental note to ask more about the car situation.

I arrived at the location before him and found a prime seat where I could see everyone approaching the bar. I wanted to spot him before he spotted me. Physically, he didn't disappoint—still just as handsome as I'd remembered. His huge smile and warm hug pulled me in; his cologne was intoxicating, and he radiated an ease I found refreshing.

He immediately went into an explanation about his car, "Don't be alarmed. I'm just having some car issues and trying to figure some stuff out."

I nodded but I was reading in between the lines. I figured his car needed some repairs and he was unable to afford them or hadn't found the right person to get them done. I was just relieved that he addressed it immediately and recognized how that could be concerning.

"I know you got it going on and ain't about to mess with no man without a car." I responded with a light laugh. "Your girl told me that you normally like a certain kind of guy and that I had to come correct."

I raised my eyebrows and said, "Mmm, what else did she tell you?"

"Aww, nothing much that I haven't already shared with you. She said you thought I was cute and she could tell I was digging you. She said you have incredibly high standards and therefore, I should consider it a privilege that you even wanted to meet me and go out."

I cringed on the inside. Jen's version of the story was that she *happened* to see him while walking her dog, casually mentioned that I thought he was cute, and passed along my number after *he* asked. But the way he was framing it? That was a whole different narrative. "What exactly did she say to you?" I probed as he ordered a drink.

He leaned in and I smelled his cologne. "She said that you rarely comment on men being attractive but with me couldn't stop talking about me and how you wanted to go out. She asked me if I would be willing to go out with you?"

"Oh, did she?" I made a mental note to smack her upside her head for lying to me.

"And she told me not to tell you that part, but I wanted to tell you how flattered I was. I like a woman who knows what she wants. And by the looks of things," he scanned me up and down and licked his lips, "I think I'm right."

I started mentally drafting the scathing speech I was going to give her. Determined to make the best of the night, I simply changed the subject. We talked about living in the Bay Area, our families, what type of music we enjoyed and some of our favorite foods. The banter was easy and light.

"You know what, all this food talk is making me hungry. Let me take you to this other spot." The night was still early and I was enjoying his company, so I agreed to extend the evening, "But you gotta drive though, I rode my bike here."

"In the cold?" I asked.

"Well, you didn't wanna pick a brotha up and I wasn't going to miss the chance to go out with you. So, yeah."

We walked to my car, trading more jokes along the way. He teased me about how small my car was and how his 6-foot-2 frame would struggle to fit inside. I fired back that it was better than the wind whipping his face as he pedaled in the cold. At the next spot, we grabbed seats at the bar and ordered some appetizers. I found myself leaning in, wanting to know more about him. Finally, I asked the question that had been circling in my mind since he first brought it up.

"So, what's the real deal with the car? Are you biking to work too?"

He went into a long, drawn-out story about how he bought the car from someone, but it has never worked properly. He wanted to fix it up but was just waiting for the right time.

Trying not to judge the man by his car situation, I decided to see what else he had to offer. "You mentioned that you normally work evenings at the restaurant. Do you normally have to work on Sundays?"

Finding out how people spend their Sundays is the single Christian equivalent of learning if someone goes to church. It's often a window into their spiritual life. While going to church isn't the only marker of faith, it usually reveals the value someone places on community, accountability, and consistent growth.

"Yeah, Sundays are busy days. We also get great tips. But when I'm not working, I normally catch up on sleep or go watch a football game or something. I've been trying to get more hours, though." I sat in silence waiting for him to share more. "I really want to be a chef or own my own restaurant. So, I'm trying to learn things from the ground up."

"That's cool. I work in retail but started out in our stores before I moved into our corporate headquarters, so I get that mentality completely. What did you do before the restaurant?"

Light-Skin Leo mentioned a fast-food chain where he worked prior to this job. "I applied at this other spot, but they required a urine test. I knew I would fail that, so I didn't even bother showing up to the orientation."

"Oh. Um . . ." I had no words. He went on to say he was living with his mom and while "trying to figure some things out," (a recurring phrase of his throughout the night) and hoping to be a manager someday. He then went on to talk about how he liked to spend his days off smoking weed, watching a game, and just chilling.

I excused myself to the bathroom. *He's cute, but he ain't it* is what I thought as I washed my hands. The false pretense of how I'd even ended up on this date, the bike-riding, and now the recreational drug use—none of it lined up with the standards I had prayed to uphold. It was a sure sign that I needed to take myself back home. I had a pair of oversized sweats and a book calling my name.

When I returned to the bar, Light-Skin Leo flashed his megawatt smile and swiveled on his bar stool, and spread his long legs to flank each side of me. In one swift move, he flung my vest open like a cowboy tossing back his trench coat and pulled me in close by wrapping his arms around my waist.

"Girl, you even smell good," he mumbled into my ear. "Probably taste good too."

I'm not going to lie to you—between his cologne, the fullness of his lips, and the swiftness of his pull, I lost all common sense for a strong thirty seconds. I threw the bike-riding, weed-smoking, and living-with-his-momma out the window and imagined entertaining Light-Skin Leo for the night. For a hot minute, I considered letting him hang around until Cuffing Season ended.

Cuffing Season may be a new term for some. It's when the need for coupleship (*new word?*) or a warm body in the cooler fall or winter weather replaces the buffoonery that once accented the summer. Days grow shorter, sweater weather[5] sets in, pumpkin lattes and hot cocoa replace margaritas, and staying in

---

5   Sweater Weather – do yourself a favor and look up "sweater weather SNL" on YouTube.

becomes far more appealing than going out. What once felt like the freedom of singleness can suddenly feel inconvenient—and cuddly nights with someone, anyone, start to look real attractive.

Cuffing Season usually kicks off with the infamous "hey stranger" or "WYD" text—or maybe a DM with a wink-face emoji to break the ice. Sometimes it's disguised as, "hey big head" or the classic, "you've been on my mind. How are you?" The beauty of this move is that it sounds casual, non-committal, and never desperate. Truth be told, the sender has likely blasted the same message to multiple people but has a preference for who they really want to respond.

Familiarity, comfort, and the need for a warm body on a cold night fuel Cuffing Season. Many people fall into it subconsciously, without even realizing it. (*Raises hand and diverts eye contact.*)

I had no doubt that while I probably would have had to drive Light-Skin Leo home afterwards, he probably could have been my warm body. He was not new to this, and it showed.

But then my common sense—aka the Holy Spirit—snapped me back into reality. I shut down the voice in my head entertaining foolishness and anchored myself in James 4:7: "Submit yourselves, then, to God. Resist the devil, and he will flee from you." I wanted to please God with my actions and date by His standards. No thrill or seasonal lovin' was worth my dignity or self-respect. And no fleeting spark was worth the regret and shame that would surely follow.

"Yeaaahhh, about that." I pulled away, straightened my vest and sat down. "I'm not sure what all Jen told you, but did she also mention that I'm celibate?"

His smile dimmed a few watts. "She said that you had some strict rules about your Christianity." *Note to self: stop hanging out with Jen.*

"Well, actually, I'm just being obedient to what the Bible says but whatevs. Point is, I'm not having sex before marriage." I try to share that fact in a lighter, more casual way, but something about this moment told me he had thought the night was headed in a very different direction.

"So, check this out," he leaned back and stroked his beard, "I ain't about that life. I don't know how you do it. I can't imagine not having sex with my girl. I respect you for it though."

"And I respect you for telling me up front that this ain't for you. Thank you." I really was appreciative that he was so straightforward with his response. While his opinion didn't matter, I appreciated his honesty far more than I would have appreciated someone ignoring my boundaries.

"Ready to call it a night?" Relief washed over me that we were on the same page—no confusion, no hard feelings.

This is the last time I purposely wear flats on a date. I wasn't sure who I was trying to prove something to. Maybe, deep down, I had started believing that my confidence and poise were the reason I was still single. I let insecurity whisper lies, entertained unworthy advice, and acted out of character. For what? To be tempted by a man I didn't even want, just so Cuffing Season wouldn't feel so lonely?

My singleness wasn't a problem to fix. And I didn't need a man, or other people's suggestions, to validate my worth. I remained fearfully and wonderfully made.

"You're cool peoples, you know that?" Light-Skin Leo put his finger in my dimple.

"So are you." And I meant that. He was fun to be around. He just wasn't someone I wanted to date.

He clapped and rubbed his hands together before saying, "I'm 'bout to go home, smoke this weed, and eat the rest of these chicken wings."

I just nodded. *Definitely made the right decision.*

I drove Light-Skin Leo back to his bike and headed home. Later that night, I received a text from Jen. I left it with the read receipt.

Not tuh-day, Satan.

Dear Lord,

Dating can be so challenging for me and my friends. It feels as if we must remain so open that we sometimes tolerate dates and circumstances that are opposite of what we prefer— because the pool of options feels so small.

I want to pray your will, and I know you will please bless me with a husband who has a meaningful relationship with you. A relationship that is already established prior to him and I meeting. Let us build together and bring you as the Head of our union. Help him to see me and help me to see him- really see him.

I hope he is sweet, genuine, and has a strong sense of family. I don't want him to smoke anything but he has to be okay with abstaining from sex (but can he have sexual stamina when it's time?). And just a few more while I'm at it—let him be confident, fun, like to try new things, and never watch porn. I pray he is ambitious, supportive of my dreams and receives support and compliments from me, lives an active lifestyle, and is a natural giver.

Even with all this Lord, help me not to create a list of what I want in a future spouse that would put boundaries on what You can/will do. Nothing is too hard for you.

Amen.

Chapter 15

What do a Salon, a Car Accident, and an Uber Driver Have in Common?

I'm convinced God added a little extra comedy to some of my dating experiences just so I'd have material for this book. That is the only way I can make sense of some of the nonsense I have encountered in this dating journey.

Case in point: Fertile Felix.

I encountered Fertile Felix during an unfortunate accident outside my beauty shop. For those who may not know, the Black beauty shop is more than just a place to get your hair done. It's culture. It's community. It's camaraderie. The Beauty Shop was a sisterhood where you could bond in psychological safety over similar lived experiences. I grew up in Beauty Shop Culture—my aunt and cousin are both licensed cosmetologists, so being at the shop weekly or biweekly was just a normal part of life.

Every week brought something new. Sometimes you sat in the lobby for what felt like forever, waiting your turn while wide-eyed kids like me watched women come and go. Beauticians doubled as therapists, prayer partners, even neighborhood reporters. They were expected to work miracles with your hair while also offering up advice, encouragement, or a good laugh.

And occasionally, something wild would happen that sent everybody out into the street mid-appointment—women with foils, suds, shower caps, rollers—you name it—out there rallying together to see what was going on. It was in one of those chaotic beauty shop moments that I met Fertile Felix. My beautician, Cherry, was trimming my ends, and we were catching up on life when a loud crash outside stopped us mid-sentence.

"Where is your car parked?" she asked.

"I'm right in front. I can see my car from here."

"Oh, okay," she paused. "Let's go outside just to make sure."

We stepped outside to find a car sitting crooked in the middle of the street. The driver looked dazed, barely coherent, and people from nearby businesses were already shouting, trying to get his attention. Before anyone could reach him, the car started to roll—straight toward my parked car.

Cherry and I both jumped up and down, arms flailing like air traffic controllers in a panic. "Nooo! No! Staaahhhppp!!"

Our screams didn't matter. His car slammed directly into mine.

The driver's head slumped against the wheel. He was unconscious, and his foot must've been pressing the gas because the tires kept spinning, smoke billowing into the air and the smell of burnt rubber filling our nostrils. "Call 911!" people yelled as they banged on the windows, trying to wake him. His doors were locked, there was no way in.

Cherry bolted for a broom handle and I fumbled for my phone, both of us praying out loud the whole way. By the time we got back, someone else had already smashed the passenger window with a tool wrapped in a towel. They reached in, unlocked the door, and half a dozen hands rushed to put the car in park and turn off the engine. "He's unconscious!" someone yelled.

"No, he's not. He's coming to!" someone else clarified. His head was bobbing up and down slightly.

"Get him some water!" another commanded.

"No, no water and don't move him!" A woman came striding over from the neighboring salon, half her hair flat-ironed, the other half clipped to the top of her head. With her cape still draped over her shoulders, she pushed through the crowd, hands waving like she owned the street. "I'm a registered nurse. Until we find out what's wrong with him, don't give him anything. The paramedics are on their way." She knelt to see if he was coherent, and he mumbled something in response to what she asked.

The nurse came over to me and asked, "Are you alright? You're abnormally calm. Are you in shock?"

I let out an awkward laugh. The last thing this situation needed was me overreacting. Thankfully, I wasn't experiencing this alone—Cherry was still by my side. She wasn't just my beautician but also a trusted member of my church community.

"Nope," I answered with a shrug. "I just want to be able to drive away and I hope he is okay."

"Okay, you sh—"

"He's throwin' up on hisself!" a young guy yelled, interrupting the nurse.

All eyes turned toward the driver who now had vomit all down the front of his beard and shirt. The faint smell of alcohol started to waft through the air.

Paramedics arrived along with a police officer. In a flurry of movement, they practically yanked the car door off its hinges to reach him. He wasn't a small man, and by the time they pulled him out, he had lost consciousness again. They laid him on the sidewalk, shirt ripped open, chest compressions underway while one medic tried to thread an IV into his toe. Medical jargon, numbers, and clipped commands filled the street.

The police officer immediately began gathering information from those who saw the first accident before he hit my car. As she talked with the witnesses, I took pictures of his license plate, his car and where the collision occurred. Eventually, someone pointed her my way. She commended me for gathering photos for my insurance claim and explained that if the driver doesn't make it, my car may be held for inspection. I blinked, nodding without fully processing. All I could manage was, "I just want to be able to drive home when this is done."

"Well, let's hope he makes it," she said before handing me a slip that included a case number and information on contacting the county courthouse. "Stick around for a bit."

Another guy joined the scene and started yelling at the driver, "This is my brother, man. Frank! Frank! Get up, man!" The paramedics continued to work on getting a pulse.

He looks so familiar. Something about his face tugged at my memory. His features weren't entirely unfamiliar. His eyes locked on mine for a moment, and I saw a flicker of recognition flash across his face too.

"How do we know him?" I asked Cherry. "Is it church?"

"I keep thinking how familiar his face is. It's not church though. C'mon girl, let me finish your hair and think about it." Since I had all the info I could possibly get for my insurance claim at the time, I followed her back in the shop to finish my trim. As she started cutting, I watched her brow furrow, then suddenly lift.

"They're twins! I grew up with them and knew their grandmother."

"Oh man. Well, I hope his brother makes it."

While I was glad that Cherry's memory had jogged loose, I still wasn't sure how I knew the guy who had just arrived on the scene. I kept racking my brain but kept coming up blank.

Once she finished, I tucked my hair into a ponytail and we went back outside. Frank was already loaded into the ambulance, and his brother—along with another man—was fussing with the crumpled car door, trying to bend it back so the car could be driven home.

"Hey, I'm so sorry this happened," Frank's brother walked up to me, looked me up and down before flashing me a crooked smile. He had a peanut-butter complexion with full lips and a stocky build. He wore dark denim jeans and an oatmeal mock-neck sweater with tan leather lace-up shoes. But it was the chunky gold pinky ring and the turquoise pendant on his chain that caught my eye. I *knew* those accessories.

"Did they say he's going to be okay?" I asked, trying not to notice the way he had checked me out as he walked up. The man's brother was in an ambulance. Surely, I was mistaken and was reading too much into his swag. He seemed to have a gravitational pull luring everyone around toward him.

"I don't know. I'm going to call his wife and head up to the hospital." I nodded in response. I could feel him still looking at me.

"Were you getting your hair done?" he asked.

"Yeah, getting a trim."

"Aww, I bet you didn't bargain for all this when you headed to the beauty shop."

"Nah, not at all."

"I can't believe I even saw this. I just happened to be driving down this street and saw my brother's car. He hangs out over here, so I figured it had to be him. I did a quick U-turn and here I am."

Before I could respond, Cherry walked up, breaking the awkward attraction I was starting to feel. "You know what . . . your grandma used to babysit me back in the day. That was your twin brother, right?"

"Yeah! I knew you looked familiar. Oh man. Small world."

"What's your name again?"

Even after learning Fertile Felix's name, I couldn't place how we knew each other but I had to say something. "You look familiar to me too. I can't put my finger on it."

"I was thinking the same thing about you," he replied, staring at me longer than necessary. "Well, let me pull this car out of the way. But don't leave before I get your contact information. I'll make sure his wife contacts you."

After he drove Frank's car to the side and I checked that mine would still start, the lightbulb went off. That's where I knew him from. We had a mutual friend. We'd met a couple of times at birthday parties she hosted. I even had a group picture in my phone to prove it—and sure enough, there he was. Fertile Felix. I shared my revelation with Cherry who had one of her own. "I know his baby momma. He has twins. They're grown now, but I don't think he was a good baby daddy, though."

I nodded and let that news knock my attraction down a few levels. I knew he was considerably older than me, which probably meant he had kids. However, hearing he had two and Cherry knew his baby momma made it a bit unappealing.

"You know what. I shouldn't have said that. I don't know that for sure so let me not put that into your head. Let me circle back with his baby momma before I go saying things I can't prove."

"Oh, it's no biggie. I ain't tripping."

"Yeah, but I saw the way he was looking at you." She cut a sly smile my way.

"So, it wasn't just me? I was thinking, surely he's not trying to get at me while his brother is headed to the hospital in an ambulance. That just seems . . . I dunno, distasteful?"

"Girl. Both of y'all dripping with swag so yeah, I bet he is attracted to you."

"It just doesn't seem right. Hold up, I'll be right back." I stepped outside to tell Fertile Felix how we knew each other. He was standing at the trunk of his car and wiping off the seat of his pants from being in Frank's car.

"Oh, no one told you about the vomit, huh?" I said as I walked up.

"Nah, and I wish I had looked first. This is gross." I couldn't help but laugh a little at the face he was making. "Let me get your number so I can check on you later and get the info over to you."

Check on me later? "Oh, you don't have to do that. You have your brother to worry about."

"Nah, I'm definitely going to call you," he said with a little more bass in his voice. He flashed that lopsided smile again. "Want to make sure you're okay." He handed me his phone.

I gave a slow nod and typed my number on the screen.

"Get home safely, Carrie."

"Thanks," I said before turning to walk back toward the salon and my car. I could feel his eyes burning into my back the whole way.

True to his word, Fertile Felix checked in a few times after that day. Always respectful, always sweet. Each time, he'd ask how I was doing, and I'd return the question about his brother. Turns out, Frank had been on his way to his girlfriend's house after leaving the bar. Both his wife and his girlfriend showed up at the hospital—so you can imagine that providing me with insurance info wasn't exactly at the top of the family's to-do list.

I let Fertile Felix know my insurance company had already handled everything, so he could stop apologizing on his brother's behalf. That should've been the end of it.

A week or two after our last conversation, he sent me a text.

> **FF:** Hey Carrie! Just checking in on you to make sure you're still doing okay.
>
> **Me:** That's sweet of you. Yep, I'm good. Thank God for insurance.
>
> **FF:** Glad to hear it. How is your week going?
>
> **Me:** It's going pretty well. Nothing too extreme. How about you?
>
> **FF:** That's wassup. My week is cool. I was thinking about you and decided to hit you up.
>
> **Me:** You were thinking about lil' ol' me?
>
> **FF:** Yeah. What do you like to do for fun?

Woah. Oh. So, this was happening. Up until now, every check-in from Fertile Felix had been quick and formal—just updates about his brother. I wasn't expecting him to slide into the personal lane. But he was cute, and I had time. Why not entertain the conversation?

I shared my love of reading, being active, writing, spending time with my church community and trying new restaurants with close friends.

FF: You don't have kids?

Me: Nope. Do you?

By now, y'all know I had already stalked this man on social media, right?

After his first three calls after the accident, I decided to see what he was all about. I was also curious about the children's situation since Cherry had also shared that he lost one of his sons in a tragic incident. I didn't see many pictures of children, but I did see pictures of his grassroots effort to support lower-income areas with healthy foods. I was just curious as to what he was willing to share.

FF: Twins. A boy and a girl.

Me: Oh, are they in the area?

FF: Yeah, just north of here.

Me: How old are they?

FF: They're grown.

Me: Ah, gotcha.

FF: You have a sec to chat?

Me: Sure.

I answered the phone with no real expectations. Obviously, Fertile Felix was interested, and I could at least appreciate that he was being upfront about it. To lighten the mood, I teased him right out the gate: "So tell me, what do you like to do besides call women you've met at the scene of an accident?"

That broke whatever awkwardness might've been lingering. We slipped into conversation easily, no longer tethered to the wreck that had brought us together.

I hinted that I had done some sleuthing online to learn a little more about him. He shared that he had tried the same but wasn't as good at it. We laughed about how we had both gone through our mutual friend for background checks—him asking about my dating status, me double-checking she hadn't dated him first.

"Well, what did you learn?" he teased.

"Nothing that has sent me running for the hills just yet. So far, your story checks out." I was sure he could hear the smile in my voice.

"I'm glad to hear that. Maybe I need to sharpen my skills. I respect that you admitted that," he said.

"Listen, every woman does it. Some of us are just better at it than others."

"You think so? Well, I still have questions for you. What do you do for a living that you ain't tripping on having car accidents? You were extra calm."

"I work well under pressure," I said, before giving him the elevator pitch on my career. He listened closely, then jumped in to share his own hustle. From running a nonprofit to driving Uber to owning a popular event space, Fertile Felix made it clear that keeping a job wasn't an issue for him. We shared what areas we live in, and he mentioned that he wasn't far away from me because he had just completed a ride in my area.

"I would ask you to link up now, but I would prefer to be more planful because I really want to take you out and get to know you better," he said.

"Okay, what were you thinking?"

"Well, I'd love to show you my event space before heading to dinner. You could park at my house then I could drive us to dinner."

Now, I could tell Fertile Felix was proud of this space, and I didn't doubt it was nice. But let me tell you what wasn't happening, me showing up at his house for a first date. I don't care how familiar we technically were or how much swag he carried. I've been around long enough to know myself—and know that his kind of swag would require a double layer of granny panties just to keep things safe.

Going back to his place and going inside for a tea or nightcap could easily lead me down a road I didn't need to travel. I knew myself, and there were too many times where my flesh silenced the warning of the Holy Spirit.

"Or I could just meet you at the spot. I don't normally get done with work until later so it would be easier just to meet you somewhere."

"Okay," Fertile Felix didn't press the issue. "I could also come to your side of town too. There's a cute spot nearby that I like called 1212 Lounge."

By this point in my dating journey, prayer had become my reflex. Therefore, I immediately prayed about the date: *Lord, let your will be done. If this is not meant to get started, don't even let us go out on a date. It's nice to be pursued but I'm not hard up for a date. I leave this in your hands.*

Some people think it's silly to involve God in *every* little decision—especially something as casual as a dinner date. But I had learned the hard way that nothing is too small for Him. If He cares about the lilies of the field, He certainly cares about who I let pursue me (Matthew 6:30).

Shortly after I prayed, Cherry sent me a text asking if I had spoken to Fertile Felix. I told her she had impeccable timing because I had just made plans to see him soon.

> **Cherry:** Did you ask him how many kids he has?
>
> **Me:** Yep, he said two—twins. A boy and girl, both grown.
>
> **Cherry:** Really? That doesn't sound right. I'm pretty sure he has more than that. Hold on.

Her text made my stomach drop. I was now on alert. While I waited for Cherry's update, I decided to launch my own little investigation. I texted our mutual friend to see if she knew how many kids he had. She wasn't sure. She knew he had been married before but never heard him mention how many children.

So, I went back to my second line of defense: social media. I was an amateur sleuth and one tagged picture could send you down a rabbit hole of cousins, baby showers, and birthday parties. I was just about to start digging when my phone lit up with Fertile Felix's name.

"I hope you aren't annoyed that I called back so soon. I enjoyed our conversation earlier and figured we could keep it going."

I politely obliged. While he expanded on the topic of gentrification that we had discussed earlier, I gave simple "mmhmms" and "yeah, that's true" in response to his comments.

"You seem a bit distracted. Did you need me to call you back?" Just as he asked, Cherry sent a text stating CALL ME in all caps.

"You know what, yeah, let me hit you back."

"No problem, do your thing."

I hung up and immediately called Cherry. She didn't bother with pleasantries.

"I knew he wasn't telling you the truth! I called his baby momma, and she said he has nine to twelve kids."

"Whaaaaattt?!" I yelled standing up from my couch. "You are kidding me."

"Nah girl. I called her because him saying he only has twins just didn't sound right. He does have twins, but he has like two to three sets of twins."

Cherry continued to explain how when this woman, Baby Momma #3, met him, he already had four kids and that's not including the son who passed away. She said he had at least two more kids after theirs if not more. She had lost count after a while considering he didn't have a great relationship with the two she had with him.

I immediately shot Fertile Felixa text asking how many kids he really had.

FF: If you're looking at my pictures, all those kids aren't mine. They were from her previous marriage.

I wasn't sure what picture he was referring to and didn't really care.

Me: You're not answering my question. How many kids do you have?

FF: Four

Me: I don't associate with liars.

FF: Who's lying?

I didn't bother responding because my prayer had been answered. I told Cherry thank you for uncovering the truth.

"I'm sorry, Carrie. I didn't mean to ruin things. I just knew he was lying and I couldn't in good conscious have access to that information and not share it with you. I prayed that if he wasn't right, it would be obvious."

"Girl, don't be sorry. You were a prompt answer to my prayer. We had just made plans to go on a date and had you not called, I would have been out with a man who apparently has the ability to impregnate women with a kiss—because my God!"

We both burst into laughter.

I continued, "No seriously. I really am glad you did some more digging. I just don't know why he would lie about that knowing that you know him and this city is as small as it is. I get it. Having a lot of kids and then stepping to someone like me with no kids is not easy. But bruh, know your lane."

"Right. He could have said, 'I've got a gang of kids.' No, you wouldn't have kept talking to him but still, what kind of man lies about how many kids he has? He has hecka kids!"

"Apparently one who has nine to twelve of them!" We erupted in laughter again.

"I'm so glad y'all didn't go out. You deserve better than that."

"I do! I also didn't realize he could breathe on me and I could get pregnant." More laughter was had before we ended the conversation, and I thanked Cherry for her honesty. I then gave thanks to God for loving me and keeping me, once again, from potential disaster.

Sure, I *could* have gone out with Fertile Felix, but what would have been the point? Any man who lies just to secure a first date is only going to keep lying. And I wasn't about to waste my time—or my prayers—on that.

I never spoke to Fertile Felix again. He was charming, yes, but I'm certain he could either make a woman very happy . . . or very pregnant. I just wasn't going to be that woman.

So, I went back to my original weekend plans of doing absolutely nothing—and found it increasingly satisfying.

Never underestimate the power of prayer in dating.

Hey Lord,

Thank you for waking me up this morning and starting me on my way. Thank you for my job and the ability to support myself out here. Unto you, oh God, do I give my life. I give you alllll my life—this includes my dating life. I surrender my will to yours.

Lord, I am seeing that there is so much purpose in this season. You are doing a new thing and I'm excited to see where it goes. I'm learning from my mistakes and resting in your mercy and grace. I know that my obedience to you is most important.

I want to ask you how long this whole single thing is supposed to last, but that seems futile now. Guide me, direct me, and help me to find complete fulfillment in you.

Thank you for your patience and grace toward me.

Amen.

Chapter 16

From Love Drought to Love Downpour

Although I wasn't new to the world of dating, there were extensive seasons where I went without a date. No one was checking for me. Not only that, but I had limited attraction toward any man, and my phone was drier than the Sahara Desert.

I called this my love drought season.

I didn't realize I was in a drought until I saw a post on social media asking, "When was the last time you went on a date?" I racked my brain and realized that not only had I not been on a date, I had not kissed a man, received a wink, flirted, or even seen any guys I was remotely attracted to in at least two years.

As I stared at that post and went to look at the comments, I honestly couldn't remember the last time I even had a man inappropriately ogle me or attempt to hit on me. Phone calls and texts from the opposite sex were non-existent. I could be at home with my phone in another room for extended periods and not worry about missing a call or notification. I hadn't even received the obligatory Cuffing Season "wyd" text from an ex.

Looking back over my drought season, I was starfishing the mess out of my bed each night in peaceful bliss. I ignored my hairy legs and ate gassy foods that would cause bloating or the loud eruptions under the covers. I was single as a pringle and not stressed about that area of my life. Contentment was the name of my game. I was thriving at work, had recently bought my first home, and was traveling regularly.

It wasn't that I didn't have time to date or that it never crossed my mind. Being in a relationship wasn't that important. There was so much change and newness happening in other areas of my life.

Next thing I knew, it had been two years since I had a romantic encounter.

It wasn't until this drought was pointed out on social media that it became an issue for me.

(Sidenote- this is reason #478 why social media is only best consumed in small doses. I was doing just fine before I saw something that reminded me of what is not happening in my life, and I had a visceral reaction to it. Protect your peace and be mindful of where you're scrolling and what you're consuming.)

I remember telling one of my sorority sisters how I had not been on a date in two years. She was shocked and reacted with multiple expletives along with a genuine question of how had I not realized it had been that long.

I didn't know how to respond. I was happy that my focus was on living life—not my relationship status—but once I realized that no one was checking for me, my singleness amplified and I felt invisible.

Sitting on the train commuting to work in the mornings or walking down the street with men of all types, I noticed that no one was meeting my eye. Men never gave me a second look—or even a first. I'm sure I might have come across as a creeper looking at all these men like they're the crazy ones for not checking me out. (*I'm also sure there is a woman suffrage leader cringing as she reads this.*)

I mistook this lack of attention from the male gaze as loneliness. Loneliness then turned into insecurity, which led to discontentment. Loneliness would haunt my thoughts, lingering on the outskirts of a memory about an unhealthy relationship. It tricked me into thinking the worst of times were the best of times.

After going so long without a date or relationship, I suddenly felt as if I was missing out on something. I lived in an amazing house with a successful career trajectory, but still I felt remorse about not having anyone to share those major life milestones with. I also wasn't feeling pretty, even though I was fit, working out regularly, and eating healthy. On top of that, fear crept in and whispered lies that finding a husband would get even harder now that I was more independent.

In my eagerness to end my love drought and erase these uncomfortable feelings, I pulled out my dry phone, brushed away the sand, and called up Entertaining Eddie.

Girl, I know. *I know.*

Even with our history, the friendship on which Entertaining Eddie and I had founded our relationship didn't completely dissolve. It was as if he had a sixth sense and knew exactly when to call. He possessed a familiarity that I mistook for comfort because he knew just what to do to make me feel beautiful and sexy again. I also liked that he was so willing to drop whatever and whomever to respond to me. He made me feel like a priority and I could pretend like I could still pull 'em (even though I wasn't pulling anything other than my inflated ego).

I am not a "stay friends with your ex" kind of person. At least, not my definition of friendship. I don't believe you can be true friends with someone you used to regularly bump pelvises with. It's too hard to avoid feelings and there's a high probability of heating things up again. I define friendship as someone I can show all sides of myself, be vulnerable, process my thoughts, and talk things through. This someone will in return, keep it real and check me on my stuff, because I value their perspective and know they are speaking from a place of godly love and genuine concern for my well-being.

Also, being friends with an ex could impact moving forward. Think about it. How could I truly build with a new boo if I was holding on to the remnants of the old one?

Entertaining Eddie and I were close acquaintances who knew how to have a good laugh or conversation. And because I had forgiven him, apologized to him for my manipulative ways, and had some growth (emphasis on *some*), I thought I could be around him and break the love drought season. I told myself I had no expectations and saw him for who he was and what he had to offer. He was a wonderful man . . . for someone else. As long as I knew that, it would just be a weekend to have fun.

Yeah right.

I was susceptible to the subtle tricks of the enemy to get me to compromise my standards and beliefs, all for the sake of fighting loneliness and insecurity.

Ignoring the consequences and being fueled by emotions doesn't work so well. Take one of my favorite Bible characters, King David. He was supposed to be at battle with his army but instead he was strolling on his rooftop one afternoon. He saw Bathsheba bathing and before we know it, King David invited Bathsheba over for a little rendezvous, got her pregnant, and then had her husband killed.

(The Bible really has the best stories.)

I was headed in the same foolish direction. I knew I had no business spending time with Entertaining Eddie but selfishly, I engaged with him because I wanted attention from a guy. I wanted to get dressed in a cute outfit and be taken out on a date.

It was all about me and what *I* wanted. This is what a minister at my church calls "belly button gazing." You're sitting there staring at your belly button and all you're thinking about and looking at is yourself.

That was me. Focusing on my feelings and gazing inward versus seeking God and asking Him to help me with my feelings and yearnings as He had in the past.

However, there was an unavoidable discomfort rumbling beneath the surface during the entire weekend I spent with Entertaining Eddie. It was as if my spirit was grieved because I was going backwards, using another man for my personal benefit, and operating outside of God's will for my life. I didn't have the familiarity of peace I had come to know and value.

Let me not forget how this decision brought unnecessary temptation to have sex. I invited the temptation into my house, let it take off its shoes, and then make itself comfortable in my bed. I selected granny panties to prevent complete foolery (and kept them on—whew!), but inviting fire into my bed and expecting to stay cool was simply not a smart decision.

And it all started with a social media post that led me to make decisions based on my feelings.

Feelings are fickle. They change all the time and have put me in some sticky situations. Whenever I hear people say things like "follow your heart," I cringe. Following your heart will have you calling up your ex because you haven't had a date in two years and want someone to rub on your booty. But the ex-encounter only reminds you why he's your ex and how nothing he says or does can fill your dating void. That is not his role and you may find yourself becoming that nine-year-old girl again in the kitchen asking if the words of a boy have any weight on your true value.

Ahem . . . I digress.

After my weekend with Entertaining Eddie, I had to check myself and ask the hard but necessary questions. Why did it matter so much to me if men were checking me out or not? Was my personal perception so shallow that it was dependent on the wondrous stare of a stranger? No wonder I was in a love drought. I was putting unnecessary weight on the opinion of others and needed to be somewhere focused on Jesus and His love for me. I had to repent for putting my desires above my obedience.

God, in his gentleness and kindness, received my repentance and reminded me how no man can provide what I should only seek Him for. When I lived a life where my feelings surrendered to the Holy Spirit, I could feel them, but they wouldn't lead my decision-making. I could talk to God about the hard times when I felt lonely and my body heated up. I could lay my burdens at His feet and take His yoke upon me. If He helped me wake up each day, exercise, and work intelligently, He could easily handle the natural desires of my body. There was no need to revert to fleeting coping mechanisms.

In hindsight, I also thought about how I represented Jesus and other Christians during that time. There I was talking about Jesus while simultaneously pushing the boundaries on sin. That was not the fruit I wanted to show for my growth in Christ. Entertaining Eddie already had a bad taste in his mouth about Jesus due to select family members parading as church folks. I didn't want my walk to add fuel to that fire.

After that lapse in judgement, I was back into love drought mode. But there was a cloud. Rain was in the forecast. The beauty about rain is that it produces mud and flowers. This love drought season morphed into something quite unexpected. Instead of looking at the time in between dates as a drought, it dawned on me that this time was quite the opposite of a love drought. It was a love downpour.

The rain I received provided the opportunity for fruit of the Spirit to grow. My hunger for God's Word grew and I became more concerned about making the most out of this season. Instead of wallowing, I began to operate with genuine joy, contentment, strong self-control, enduring patience and faithfulness.

Instead of saying things like, "when I get married I will," I started saying, "I'm glad I get the opportunity to do this now." It may sound silly in this modern day, but my mind concocted lies about the ability to achieve certain life milestones as a single woman living in California. I thought I would have to save buying a home or traveling internationally for marriage. It never occurred to me that God wanted me to live a full life and have abundant experiences with Him in my single season.

Be it a beautiful trip to Johannesburg with other girlfriends in similar areas of life, working part-time as a stylist to help rebuild my savings account after the purchase of my home, or making strategic career moves that opened up other doors of personal development—the rain drenched my landscape and I began living my life. A full, inspiring life.

I was a living, walking, talking blessing (cue the shouting music).

Nowhere in the Bible does it say you can't have an abundant life as a single woman. Nowhere does it say you have to save special moments for when you are partnered. Nowhere—and I mean nowhere—does it say you can't have a fulfilling life without a spouse.

My church community also began to show up as family. One Sunday while walking to my seat, I stopped and talked with four to five people, exchanged hugs and felt a smile permanently affixed to my face. This was new since I was normally late to Sunday morning service and left as soon as the closing prayer wrapped up. I was scared to make connections because I didn't feel "holy enough" to build community. But as I grew in the rain, I found myself calendaring other community-building activities at the church like women's movie night or singles ministry events—things I had deemed as silly before but now looked forward to.

My team at work became another resource for fun and laughter. Those are not normally two words associated with coworkers but a purposeful connection with three other single women of diverse backgrounds along with my married boss gave me some of the biggest laughs and best workdays I could imagine. Having this amazing crew of coworkers was especially important because as a single person, I was guilty of idolizing career accomplishments when other personal areas of my life weren't going as planned.

Instead of grumbling or complaining to my office mates, we laughed. We teased one another. We challenged and supported one another. We ate amazing food and danced together.

Not only was I learning to love my life and experience contentment at my job with the same nine-year-old confidence I once embodied, I learned to love God in the most intimate, sweet, and gentle way. And through the lens of His love, life came alive. Rain watered the seeds in my life and they grew with vibrant colors of joy, self-control, kindness, and patience. As I spent more time with God's Word, I started to regularly feel that mushy tingle of being loved, loving all the many pieces of me, and knowing how to love others with that awareness.

It was in this downpour, God restored my desire to write, and my blog was birthed. Creativity flowed through my fingertips along with wisdom and revelation of my greater purpose in serving His kingdom.

Won't. He. Do. It.

Chapter 17

Don't Settle for Saul

Compromise has lingered at the edge of nearly every romantic relationship I've attempted in my adult life. The Holy Spirit would direct me in my decision-making, but the fear of the unknown, or fear of loneliness would try to seduce me into settling for less than God's best in my life.

I'd seen it happen before. People grew tired of waiting and said yes to the wrong "yes". One person married to avoid loneliness only to feel lonelier within the marriage. Another stayed with someone because having *anyone* seemed easier than learning to stand on their own—even if that meant living in constant drama, anxiety, and trauma. Still others deferred their God-given gifts and callings for relationships that drained their creativity and buried their purpose.

One day at a women's service, God gave me a new perspective on settling. I was thirsty for a word from Him—still in my season of singleness and weary from the emotions that swirled around my unmet desires. Each month's gathering always gave me something to chew on, but that morning, I knew God had something specifically for me.

Minister Kay, affectionately known as MK, was the teacher that morning. She led the women's ministry from a refreshingly transparent perspective grounded in the truth of God's word. She always spoke truth to the ladies and addressed the hard topics that some churches have been known to ignore.

MK anchored her lesson in Deuteronomy 17:14-20, Israel's guidelines for a King. God was instructing them on what a king should be. He knew the Israelites would look around at other nations and want what they had. They'd measure themselves by comparison instead of trusting His direction.

She immediately had my undivided attention. Comparison had reared its ugly head through recent conversations with friends. Old friends would call asking, *"What's new?"* but what they really wanted to know was if I had an update in the love department. When I didn't, the energy in the conversation deflated. Some would quickly fill the silence by sharing their racy stories—new dates, flings, or what they hoped was the "real thing." Meanwhile, I was at home painting my nails on Saturday nights and bingeing YouTube sermons.

In Deuteronomy, God knew the Israelites would play the game of comparison and desire a King. In his graciousness, he gave them guidelines. At the top of the list was the King must be chosen by the Lord.

Tears pricked my eyes. I was waiting on God to send me my king. *I'd love for Him to choose someone, but it just seems to be taking a really long time.*

God also said the King should not build up large stable of horses for himself nor marry many wives because they would turn his heart from God.

I took this to understand that my king couldn't be greedy or self-righteous and would need to value his covenant with one woman.

God then shared that the king must copy the word of God in the presence of the Levitical priests and keep that copy with him, reading it every day as long as he lives. This daily devotion would protect him from pride and remind him that he was not above his people.

My interpretation was that my future king would have to be a man willing and dedicated to following the word of God every day of his life. A man confident in who he is, but humble enough to submit to God's authority. Someone with strength that didn't come from ego, but from reverence for the Lord.

From there, MK turned us to 1 Samuel 8, where Israel's desire for a king came to life. Even after being told what kind of king they needed, the elders still demanded Samuel appoint one so they could be "like all the other nations."

This was hitting home, like standing on my own doorstep, ringing the doorbell. While I hadn't demanded God to give me anything, I petitioned regularly for him to send me a man. There were times I even added a "but you did it for so-n-so" plea mingled in with my "Why am I the only one who has to wait?" Instead of thanking Him for His provision and learning to wait with contentment, I was guilty of asking for more of His *hand* than His *heart*.

MK went on to explain that the Israelites did the same thing. They were so adamant about having a king, they refused to wait on God's timing or follow His guidelines. So, God gave Samuel permission to anoint Saul as king. In essence, God gave them exactly what they were asking for. This may seem like a good thing, but every good thing isn't a God-thing.

Samuel warned the people what their demand would cost them. The king they wanted so badly would draft their sons to ride his chariots, while others would be forced to plow his fields. Some would be assigned to forge weapons and equipment. Their daughters would be taken to cook, bake, and make perfumes for him. After stripping families of their freedom, this king would eventually come after their land and crops, redistributing them to his officials. In other words, "This will be your king, but you'll regret it."

Whew. Talk about being careful what you ask for.

MK walked up and down the middle aisle of the classroom, teaching about the flaws of Saul and how the Israelites' impatience and desires led them down the wrong path. They were more focused on the trap of comparison than on the word of God. At one point, she locked eyes with me—and I'm positive she saw it. She saw the weight of my waiting, the temptation to settle. Because honestly? Sometimes it felt easier to entertain a Saul than wait for a David. My head dropped as I wondered if I even had the patience for a King David. The Israelites were so busy demanding to have a king, they couldn't wait to see how God already had one in mind. He was already raising up David, a man after His own heart, who was in the field shepherding his father's sheep and goats. While Saul was hiding from his responsibility and avoiding his ordination, David was already on the scene, being prepared to learn how to guard the sheep of the pasture. He was fearlessly defending them from the claws of the bear and jaw of the lion.

This was the king God had planned for His people.

I'm not knocking the Israelites though. I get it. Waiting for the king God had for me that met His criteria seemed impossible. I'm positive they felt like waiting for a King seemed just as futile.

Men who were attractive *and* loved the Lord *and* walked with the fruit of the Spirit? Add in "gainfully employed," "kind," and "knew how to treat a woman"? That felt like asking for a unicorn. Settling started to feel more realistic than waiting—at least then I could have what I thought I wanted. As MK shared her own testimony about how desire clouded her judgment in her marriage, she hit us with the lesson, "Don't settle for Saul! Don't settle for the counterfeit king just because you think it meets your desires. God is already preparing His best for you and has it planned to come your way in His timing."

Shen then went on to share why many settle for Saul, "Number one, you settle for Saul because you want to be like everyone else. You see what other people have and want it for yourself."

Nail. On. Head. Tears burned in my eyes. It was as if she knew my thoughts from afar off. God must have told her this lesson was for Carrie. Part of my reason for wanting to settle was because I wanted a relationship and was tired of being alone. I wanted to be invited to the couple's dinner or have a plus one to the event. I couldn't wait to have the exciting update about my dating life when a friend called to catch up.

MK continued with the second reason people settle for Saul: because they are dissatisfied with their current circumstances and walking in discontentment.

"Pray, 'Lord, help me appreciate my current season and walk in joy,'" she instructed.

I whispered the prayer with sincerity. My life was good. I didn't want a mediocre marriage. God had blessed me to abound in so many areas of my life. The last thing I wanted to do was to make Him think I was ungrateful as if all the goodness He had poured into my life was not enough because I still wanted *this one thing*.

The next reason why many settled for Saul hit hard. "You will settle for Saul if you refuse to obey the word of God." She explained that God will not send a godly woman a man who has no desire to have a relationship with Him.

She wasn't wrong. A godly woman won't receive a man from God who doesn't even want a relationship with Him. In other words, if I claimed to love Jesus, why would I think He'd hand me someone who didn't? My king couldn't be a man chasing "good vibes" or "the universe." And he definitely couldn't be someone who left no consistent trail of the Spirit's fruit behind him. If he was rude, disruptive to my peace, selfish, or allergic to sacrifice—homeboy had to go.

She went on to share how many people fall into the idea of settling because they don't believe Jesus is enough. The Israelites wanted a man, a king, to go out and fight their battles for them. They didn't fully trust that God, in His sovereignty, could do it for them.

I knew the "right" Christian answer. Of course He's enough. But if I was honest in that moment, my real answer was murkier.

Like the Israelites, I wanted someone tangible—a man to touch, hold, laugh with, and lean on. Did I believe God could be the best husband, the truest friend, the lover of my soul? I didn't truly believe it at the time. I needed the Lord to show me. I was eager to know what it meant for Him to be enough for me. I wasn't asking Him to prove it. I just needed Him to show me *how* He is enough.

MK's last reason why some settle for Saul was lack of surrender: "Your will cannot override God's will for your life." She looked at each of us in that room and explained how we must be willing to surrender our plans, our agenda to God and not operate on this invisible timetable we have created.

As someone who likes to outline and make plans about what I want God to do in my life, this was a hard one to digest.

So, I'm just supposed to give up my plans? I thought.

But the truth is, surrender *was* the plan all along. Giving up my will wasn't a punishment—it was an invitation. The same God who created me is wise enough, strong enough, and good enough to direct my path. He doesn't just know my story; He's writing it, line by line, even in the frustrating and confusing chapters. MK also made it clear not to confuse settling with expecting perfection, and how I shouldn't shoot down everyone under the guise of settling. She reminded us that marriage is not about two flawless people magically fitting together—it's about two imperfect people willing to compromise, stretch, and extend grace in order to glorify God through their union.

Thoughts whirled around in my mind at warp speed. Every word, every lesson, and every point felt so relevant and so alive. I looked around the room to see if this revelation had hit anyone else the way it had me. I imagine Jesus and my angels were standing back and smiling at me because they saw this truth taking root in my heart.

Just as I thought I was ready to close my Bible, MK had us turn to Luke chapter six to read verses 46-48 so we could learn how to overcome the temptation to settle.

There's more? I was feeling a bit overwhelmed yet hopeful. This was a lot to digest but there was biblical evidence associated with my struggles. I was being handed the exact biblical framework for why I struggled with settling—and more importantly, how to overcome it.

In Luke 6:46-48, Jesus is teaching on the parable of two foundations. The passage described two builders: one who dug deep and laid his foundation on the rock, and another who built on shifting sand. When the storm came, only the house with the firm foundation stood.

MK connected the dots plainly: *If you don't want to settle for Saul, you've got to build differently.* That means digging deep, examining the parts of your old nature that need to go, and laying your foundation on Christ alone. I couldn't be around here fornicating and living like everyone else yet expecting God to send me a godly man. That's not how it worked.

I'd have to dig deep, develop a consistent prayer life, and spend time in God's Word so I could learn more about His character. Once I did the work to dig deeper, I could lay the right foundation. In the laying, there was a chance the elements would beat and weather me, but my foundation would remain sound.

That Saturday, as I walked to my car with tear-stained cheeks, the rays from the sun warmed me from the inside out. I felt worthy of His love and confident that my singleness was part of His divine plan. He didn't want me settling for the many Sauls that had already crossed my path.

"Don't settle for Saul" echoed through my mind when I faced what I thought was the answer to prayer. I had reconnected with a childhood acquaintance and struck up a fast-moving romance with Towering Tyler. (He was 6'4". *Need I say more?*)

At first, he seemed to check all the boxes. We both loved Jesus. The relationship moved fast, maybe too fast, and for a moment I thought, *Finally, God has sent my king.* But soon the cracks showed. Our expectations clashed, our conflict styles collided, and it became clear, not only were we on different pages, Towering Tyler and I weren't even reading from the same book. If I said left, he said right. If I said up, he said down. I was eager to make this work, but I couldn't deny the truth: he wasn't God's best for me. He was emotionally unavailable, and I was not about to settle for lackluster love.

I chose to walk away—abruptly, without closure, and without explanation. I chose to stand on the firm foundation of God's Word. I believed my Author had already written a better chapter. Settling was not an option. I hadn't waited all that time to feel unloved, unseen, and unvalued.

Heartbroken and confused, I didn't give up hope. I believed God had someone so right for me, it would astonish me. Until that king came along, I would work to ignore the trap of comparison, refuse the lies of the enemy, and surrender my desires to the King of Kings. My commitment was simple: stay prayed up, stay in the Word, and stay accountable to wise counsel.

From the butterflies of Rapping Richard to the date-dodging of Fertile Felix, every interaction left me with gifts and lessons. I would not be tempted to settle for a warm body, a fancy dinner, or an unholy booty rub.

Dating counter-culturally and believing my love story was being written by the greatest Author of all time meant there would be times when I felt different, odd, or weird. But I'd rather be weird every day than end up in a desperate, unhappy, regret-filled marriage because I chose Saul when David was just around the corner.

Until that better king came along, I'd keep submitting every man who crossed my path back to God.

And I'd keep encouraging others to wait well in their single season too.

Here's to being astonished.

Epilogue

If my single season taught me anything, it's that God's ways are not my ways, and His timing is not my timing (*no matter how much I petitioned to expedite His plan*).

Never did I imagine that at the age of 41, I would have a tennis coach who became a friend . . . that at 42 I'd start dating that coach . . . and that at 44 I'd marry him. It's love grounded not just in attraction, but friendship and faith.

Lovable Luis, patient with my tennis tantrums and pitiful backhand, was the kind of guy who quietly showed up for people without making a big fuss. He became a consistent presence-kind, steady and only slightly awkward. At first, I dismissed him as a sweet, quiet guy who wasn't my type. I even joked about finding him a woman who would appreciate his low-key approach to life.

I saw him around church but never realized he had been observing me with the same curiosity I had brushed off in him. A few conversations and one awkward-but-charming brunch later, I started to notice details I'd missed—the depth of his faith, the thoughtfulness in his words, and his subtle but intentional pursuit to grow as a man of God. When he confessed during a tennis rally that he found me intimidating but valued my heart for God, it flipped a switch in me.

What began as tennis banter and light-hearted friendship slowly shifted into meaningful conversations and shared vulnerabilities about God, life, and relationships. Lovable Luis wasn't just the quiet tennis guy anymore; he was someone who could match my boldness with quiet strength.

It turns out God had been orchestrating our tennis volleys, awkward conversations, and mutual misjudgments into a storyline that was only just beginning.

God, in His sovereignty, took me the long way to the altar. And I am forever grateful that He did. I can confidently say that I was not ready for marriage at the time I desired it most (as you probably gathered if you've read to this point).

Today, I wear my granny panties for comfort instead of boundaries—but trust me, the drawer isn't closed. There are still revelations to uncover, growth to stretch into, and maybe even a few surprises tucked between those seams.

God is still writing my love story, one line at a time.

Acknowledgements

Writing and publishing a book is no easy feat, and I am forever grateful for all those who supported, encouraged, and prayed me through this journey.

I always joke that I'm an old church woman with mints in her purse, so let me give praise and honor to my Lord and Savior, Jesus Christ. This book wouldn't exist without His love, inspiration, and creativity. I didn't see what He was doing then, but I'm grateful for every single experience. He truly is the Giver of good gifts.

Next, I have to thank my incredible husband, Luis. Thank you for inspiring me to step outside of my comfort zone to publish this book. Thanks for giving me space to edit and revise, even when it meant missing a few outings and activities. The Lord knew what He was doing when He gave me you. I love and appreciate you more than words can say.

Major love to my parents and my sister. Thank you for every prayer, every encouraging word, and every scripture you sent to support me along the way. Y'all saw this when it was only a dream, and your belief in me (along with your faith-filled prayers) kept me going. And of course, my brother—I'll never forget the perfectly timed memes about waiting on God or the ones just to make me laugh.

To my dear friend Rhianwen—thank you for sending food on those days I barely left the house while writing. You reminded me I didn't have to do it all alone. Minister Kathryn, thank you for being such a thoughtful beta reader and for pouring so much wisdom into me. I love you greatly. To each of my girlfriends who cheered me on in this self-publishing journey—your encouragement reminded me to keep pressing forward when the road felt long.

A special thank you to my editors: Karen Beattie, my content editor from More to the Story, for helping me sharpen my message. I am very grateful to Mikaeal Mathews for streamlining everything so beautifully. Your expertise brought this book to life in a way I could not have done on my own.

Finally, to every friend, prayer partner, and reader who has supported me in ways both big and small—thank you. I pray this book blesses you as much as it blessed me to write it.

www.ingramcontent.com/pod-product-compliance
Lightning Source LLC
Chambersburg PA
CBHW050902160426
43194CB00011B/2258